CW01625342

# NUTRITION FOR MEN OVER 40

## How to Naturally Boost Testosterone, Lose Weight, Build Muscle, and Increase Energy

FUNK ROBERTS

**Nutrition for Men Over 40: How to Naturally Boost Testosterone, Lose Weight, Build Muscle, and Increase Energy**

Published by Funk Roberts Publishing
Toronto, Canada

Copyright © 2023 by Funk Roberts. All rights reserved.

No part of this book may be reproduced in any form or by any mechanical means, including information storage and retrieval systems without permission in writing from the publisher/author, except by a reviewer who may quote passages in a review.

All images, logos, quotes, and trademarks included in this book are subject to use according to trademark and copyright laws of the United States of America.

ISBN: 978-1-7390789-0-4
HEALTH & FITNESS / Men's Health

Cover and interior design by Victoria Wolf, wolfdesignandmarketing.com, copyright owned by Funk Roberts

Cover photo by Dawn Bowman of D.C. Bowman Photography

All rights reserved by Funk Roberts Publishing.
Printed in the United States of America.

This book is designed to provide information for men who are 40 years and older only. It is sold with the understanding that the publisher and author are not engaged in rendering medical, legal, financial or other professional services. If professional services or expert assistance is required, the services of a specialist should be sought.

Because of rapid changes in the industry, this book contains information on nutrition, recovery tips, sleep advice and workouts as of press time. Therefore, this text should be used only as a general guide and not as the ultimate source of information for this subject.

Marc "Funk" Roberts, or anyone associated with Funk Roberts Fitness Ltd advises readers to take full responsibility for their safety and know their limits. Before partaking in the exercises in this or any other program, be sure that your equipment is well maintained, and do not take risks beyond your level of experience, aptitude, training, and fitness.

Please discuss all nutritional changes with your physician or a registered dietitian. If your physician recommends that you don't use this or any other program, please follow your doctor's orders.

The purpose of this book is to educate and guide men over 40 to live a healthier lifestyle. The author shall have neither liability nor responsibility to any person or entity with respect to any loss or damage caused, or alleged to have been caused, directly or indirectly, by the information contained in this book.

# Contents

**THE AWAKENING:** Funk's Story ..... xv

**INTRODUCTION:** Ready to Prioritize Your Health and Fitness? ..... xix

**SECTION 1: UNDERSTANDING NUTRITION AND TESTOSTERONE**

**CHAPTER 1:** Why the Meta-Test Boost Nutrition System? ..... 1

**CHAPTER 2:** Testosterone and Food – What You Must Know ..... 11

**CHAPTER 3:** Nutrition 101 – Macronutrient Primer ..... 17

**CHAPTER 4:** Calories and Testosterone ..... 27

**SECTION 2: OPTIMIZING NUTRITION FOR TESTOSTERONE PRODUCTION**

**CHAPTER 5:** Testosterone-Boosting Superfoods ..... 31

**CHAPTER 6:** The Power Micronutrients for Optimal Testosterone Production ..... 37

**CHAPTER 7:** How Hydration Factors into Your Overall Health ..... 43

**CHAPTER 8:** Foods That Are Crushing Your Testosterone Levels ..... 47

SECTION 3: IMPLEMENTING THE META-TEST BOOST NUTRITION SYSTEM

CHAPTER 9: Welcome to the Meta-Test Boost Nutrition System 28-Day Meal Plan ........ 57

CHAPTER 10: The 10 Commandments of the Meta-Test Boost Nutrition System ........ 67

CHAPTER 11: Food List for a Healthy, Testosterone-Boosting Eating Plan ........ 73

CHAPTER 12: Do-It-Yourself Meal Plan ........ 83

CHAPTER 13: Done-For-You Meal Plan ........ 89

SECTION 4: SUCCESS STORIES

CONCLUSION: Taking Control of Your Health and Fitness ........ 117

Science and Research References ........ 119

Dedication ........ 123

Acknowledgments ........ 125

About the Author ........ 127

# Before and After

OVER 40 ALPHA
FOR MEN
BEFORE
AFTER

BEFORE
OVER 40 ALPHA
FOR MEN
AFTER

OVER 40 ALPHA
FOR MEN
BEFORE
AFTER
WWW.OVER40ALPHA.COM

BEFORE
OVER 40 ALPHA
FOR MEN
AFTER

BEFORE
OVER 40 ALPHA
FOR MEN
AFTER

BEFORE
OVER 40 ALPHA
FOR MEN
AFTER

OVER 40 ALPHA
FOR MEN
WWW.OVER40ALPHA.COM
before
after

BEFORE
OVER 40 ALPHA
FOR MEN
AFTER

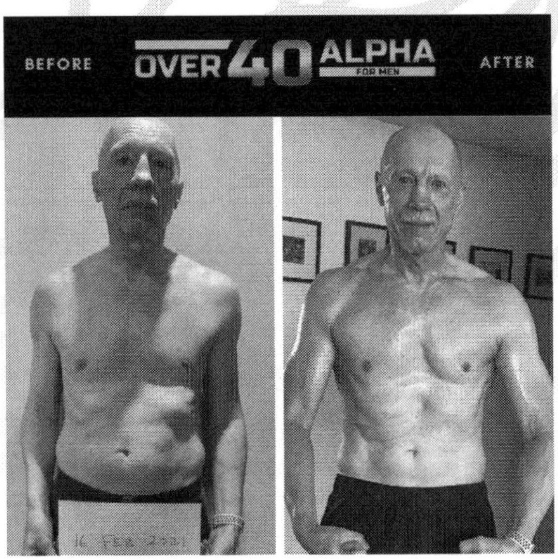
BEFORE
OVER 40 ALPHA
FOR MEN
AFTER

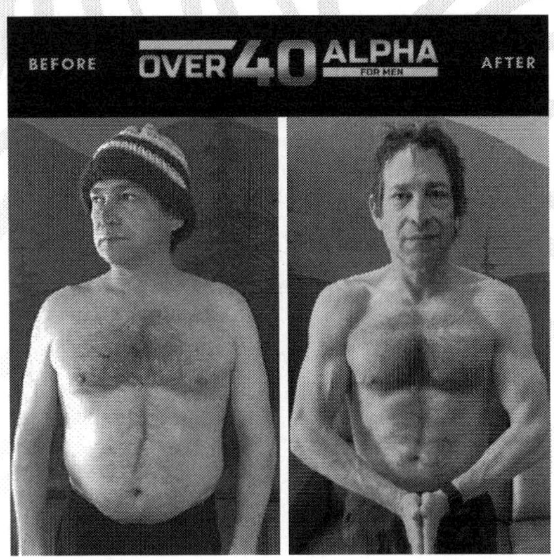
BEFORE
OVER 40 ALPHA
FOR MEN
AFTER

BEFORE
OVER 40 ALPHA
FOR MEN
AFTER

BEFORE
OVER 40 ALPHA
FOR MEN
AFTER

BEFORE
OVER 40 ALPHA
FOR MEN
AFTER

BEFORE
OVER 40 ALPHA
FOR MEN
AFTER
5TH JAN 2019

BEFORE
OVER 40 ALPHA
FOR MEN
AFTER

BEFORE
OVER 40 ALPHA
FOR MEN
AFTER

BEFORE
OVER 40 ALPHA
FOR MEN
AFTER

BEFORE
OVER 40 ALPHA
FOR MEN
AFTER

BEFORE
OVER 40 ALPHA
FOR MEN
AFTER

BEFORE
OVER 40 ALPHA
FOR MEN
AFTER

OVER 40 ALPHA
FOR MEN
BEFORE
AFTER
WWW.OVER40ALPHA.COM

BEFORE
OVER 40 ALPHA
FOR MEN
AFTER

BEFORE
OVER 40 ALPHA
FOR MEN
AFTER

BEFORE
OVER 40 ALPHA
FOR MEN
AFTER

BEFORE
OVER 40 ALPHA
FOR MEN
AFTER

BEFORE
OVER 40 ALPHA
FOR MEN
AFTER
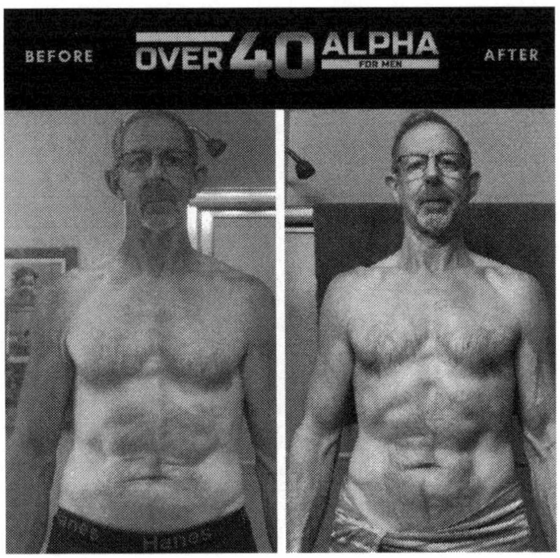
BEFORE
OVER 40 ALPHA
FOR MEN
AFTER
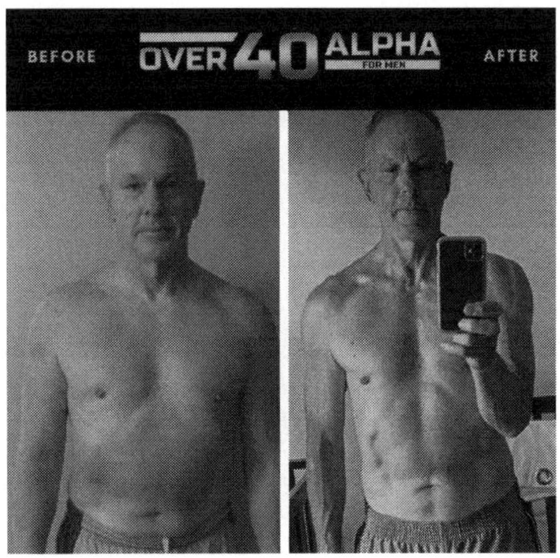
BEFORE
OVER 40 ALPHA
FOR MEN
AFTER

# THE AWAKENING
## Funk's Story

**FUNK ROBERTS,** a former professional athlete and renowned master metabolic trainer, recounts his remarkable journey to becoming the leading authority on nutrition for men over 40. Through a series of life-altering events and struggles, he discovered the crucial role that nutrition plays in men's health and well-being.

Funk's career as a professional beach and indoor volleyball player spanned two decades, taking him around the world and teaching him how to train at the highest level. However, as he entered his 30s and retired from professional sports, Funk transitioned into a corporate lifestyle. While maintaining his passion for fitness and dabbling in personal training, his focus shifted toward providing for his family.

By the age of 39, Funk's life took a turn. Here's his story.

"Despite consistently going to the gym, I found it increasingly difficult to build muscle and shed excess weight. My energy levels and mood began to suffer, and I even lost my sex drive. It was during this trying period that my relationship with my girlfriend fell apart, and my training partner challenged me to confront my stagnant progress. This confrontation served as a wake-up call and set me on a new path.

"Desperate for change, I tried numerous workout routines and diets but found little success. My downward spiral led to injuries, depression, and a reliance on unhealthy coping mechanisms. Eventually, I visited a doctor who determined my testosterone levels were alarmingly low.

"Refusing testosterone replacement therapy, I instead sought natural ways to boost my testosterone levels. Through diligent research, I consulted with fitness experts and was surprised to discover that nutrition held the key. By transforming my diet and focusing on recovery and stress management, I managed to revitalize my health and lose 30 pounds by the time I turned 40.

"Emboldened by this success, I founded two companies, got married, overcame addiction, and made a name for myself in the fitness industry. By targeting strength training for MMA and combat athletes, I became the go-to expert for helping fighters achieve peak physical condition.

"However, I faced another significant obstacle at 48 when I was diagnosed with cryptogenic organizing pneumonia. This life-threatening lung disorder severely impaired my breathing and left me on the brink of death. Thankfully, after a successful surgery and a challenging recovery process, I was able to bounce back.

"My unwavering commitment to my nutritional plan played a vital role in my recovery. My focus on balanced meals that are rich in complex carbs, high-quality proteins, healthy fats, and vegetables and fruits continues to help me maintain and even increase my testosterone levels. I firmly believe that nutrition is the foundation for optimal health and well-being.

"Through my experience, I realized that traditional nutrition plans were not tailored for the unique needs of men over 40. Therefore, I developed a sustainable and straightforward nutrition system that thousands of men worldwide have successfully adopted. The program emphasizes the importance of a balanced diet and encourages participants to enjoy their favorite foods while improving their health. "I am humbled by the support and caring I see every day with the men in my program – my brothers – and am extremely proud of them and their accomplishments."

Funk's story serves as an inspiring testament to the transformative power of proper nutrition. He overcame immense adversity by focusing on the fundamental role nutrition plays in building muscle, losing weight, fighting chronic diseases, balancing hormones, and boosting mood.

His message is one of hope and determination, encouraging men to take the first step toward a healthier lifestyle, no matter their current state. By embracing the right nutrition system, men over 40 can look and feel their best while becoming the healthiest version of themselves.

As Funk Roberts confidently declares, "It's time for you to get it done!"

# INTRODUCTION
# Ready to Prioritize Your Health and Fitness?

**ARE YOU A MAN OVER THE AGE OF 40** who is struggling to maintain your health and fitness goals?

Do you have trouble getting rid of belly fat?

Does it feel like no matter what you do, you can't seem to lose weight, build muscle, or improve your energy levels?

Are you confused about what foods to eat, when to eat, and how much to eat on a daily basis?

Are you totally confused by all the nutritional information you read online, in magazines, on social media, or even that your friends and family tell you?

## Brother, You Are Not Alone!

Many men over the age of 40, 50, 60, and beyond face the same challenges when it comes to nutrition and health, which can make it difficult to achieve their goals.

The aging process impacts men's bodies in various ways, and without a targeted approach men can struggle to achieve and maintain their health and fitness goals.

One of the main challenges that aging men battle is the decline of testosterone levels. As men age, their testosterone levels naturally decrease 1 to 2 percent each year after the age of 40. This leads to a loss of muscle mass, weight gain, decreased energy, and decreased sex drive.

These changes can be frustrating and can impact men's self-confidence and overall well-being.

Additionally, men over 40 are at a higher risk of developing chronic health conditions, such as heart disease, diabetes, and cancer. These conditions can be exacerbated by poor nutrition and eating habits, leading to more serious health consequences.

Moreover, men over 40 are more likely to experience more inflammation and joint pain, which can limit the ability to exercise and engage in everyday activities.

Finally, men over 40 often experience more and more stress in both their personal and professional lives, which has a huge impact on mental health and mood and often leads to depression. High levels of stress can lead to poor sleep, unhealthy eating habits, and an increased risk of chronic health conditions.

To make matters worse, many men who are challenged with declining hormone levels are struggling to burn fat and lose weight, are seeing an increased risk of chronic health conditions, are feeling more joint aches and pains, and may be experiencing a higher level of stress.

Does this sound familiar to you? Then, as I mentioned before, you are not alone, but you are not off the hook! Because as a *man*, you are put on this earth to *provide*, *protect*, and *procreate*.

Staying fit and healthy is of the utmost importance, as you are traditionally seen as the main provider, protector, and procreator for your family, and you cannot be all that if you are unhealthy, obese, and in a hospital bed suffering from chronic illness.

Maintaining physical and mental wellness enables you to be a better father, husband, son, brother, grandfather, and leader in your community.

Regular exercise, good sleep habits, post-workout recovery strategies, and a balanced nutrition lifestyle will not only help improve your overall health but will also CRUSH the challenges you may be facing right now.

And the one factor that has the greatest impact on your health as you age is NUTRITION!

When you follow the right, targeted approach to nutrition, specifically designed for your age, you will transform your body while maintaining your health and fitness, so you can live a healthy and fulfilling life and be the alpha man that you were created to be.

## I Call This Targeted Approach and Solution the Meta-Test Boost Nutrition System

My revolutionary nutrition and lifestyle program, backed by science and research, is specifically designed to help men like you over the age of 40 lose belly fat, improve energy, naturally increase testosterone levels, boost metabolism, build muscle, reduce weight, and improve overall health in just 28 days.

And now, with this book, you will learn my step-by-step, simple-to-follow nutrition plan – and lifestyle – and how it can help you achieve your health and fitness goals as you age.

The Meta-Test Boost Nutrition System is based on the principles of natural, whole foods and emphasizes the right mix of complex carbs, healthy fats, proteins, and veggies/fruits that will naturally increase your testosterone production, build lean muscle, balance your hormones, and rev up your fat-burning metabolism while supplying you with more daily energy and better overall health.

Why do I call my nutrition system Meta-Test Boost? Because this system empowers you to naturally boost your *metabolism* and *testosterone.*

Unlike many other diets that focus on calorie restriction or cutting out food groups, the Meta-Test Boost Nutrition System provides a sustainable and effective approach to nutrition that is specifically tailored to your needs as a man over 40.

As you read this book, you'll see that my goal is to educate you on nutrition and not just have you follow another diet.

The more you understand why you need to eat certain foods, why you need to stay away from certain foods, and how nutrition affects your overall hormonal balance, decreases inflammation, and fuels your body on a daily basis, the easier it will be for you to grasp this simple nutrition plan, so you can immediately implement this into your life as soon as you finish the book.

## This Will Be the Last Nutrition Plan You Will Ever Need!

Here's what you can expect to find in this book:

In Section 1, you will gain a foundational understanding of how nutrition and testosterone impact men's health and fitness.

Chapter 1 introduces the benefits of the Meta-Test Boost Nutrition System, including increased testosterone levels, improved metabolism, muscle building, weight loss, and overall health. This chapter delves into the principles behind the Meta-Test Boost Nutrition System and why it is uniquely suited for men over 40.

Chapter 2 explores the critical relationship between testosterone and food, explaining how specific foods can impact testosterone production.

In Chapter 3, you will receive a detailed overview of macronutrients, including carbohydrates, proteins, and fats, and how they can impact testosterone production.

Chapter 4 addresses the important topic of calorie intake and testosterone production, offering guidance on how much food to consume for optimal results.

*By the end of Section 1, you will have a clear understanding of the foundational principles of nutrition and testosterone and how they relate to the Meta-Test Boost Nutrition System.*

Section 2 focuses on optimizing nutrition for testosterone production.

Chapter 5 provides an overview of testosterone-boosting superfoods and their role in the Meta-Test Boost Nutrition System. You will learn about foods such as oysters, eggs, and avocados that are packed with nutrients that can help increase testosterone production.

Chapter 6 delves into micronutrients, such as vitamins and minerals, and their important role in optimal testosterone production.

In Chapter 7, you will learn about the importance of hydration and how it can impact testosterone production.

Chapter 8 addresses foods that can negatively impact testosterone levels, such as processed foods, soy, and sugar and provides guidance on how to avoid them.

*By the end of Section 2, you will have a detailed understanding of how to optimize your nutrition for maximum testosterone production and overall health.*

In Section 3, you will receive a comprehensive guide to implement the Meta-Test Boost Nutrition System.

Chapter 9 introduces the 28-day meal plan, which includes guidance on how to structure meals for optimal results.

Chapter 10 provides Meta-Test Boost Nutrition System's 10 Commandments, which are key principles to keep in mind as you follow the program.

In Chapter 11, you will receive a comprehensive food list, including recommended foods to eat and those to avoid.

Finally, Chapters 12 and 13 provide detailed guidance on how to structure your meals throughout the day for maximum impact on testosterone production and overall health. Chapter 12 presents a Do-It-Yourself Meal Plan, while Chapter 13 provides an easy-to-follow, 28-day Done-For-You Meal Plan.

*By the end of Section 3, you will have all the tools and knowledge you need to implement the Meta-Test Boost Nutrition System and achieve optimal results.*

In Section 4, you will have the opportunity to learn from real-life success stories of men over 40 who have used the Meta-Test Boost Nutrition System to transform their health and fitness. Through a collection of inspiring and motivating stories, you will learn about the specific benefits these men achieved, including weight loss, muscle gain, and improved energy levels. Additionally, you will gain insights into the individual challenges they faced and how they overcame them to achieve success with the program.

These success stories will inspire and motivate you to take action toward your own health and fitness goals and give you a sense of the possibilities that lie ahead when you commit to the Meta-Test Boost Nutrition System.

Are you ready?

**LET'S GOOOOOOOOOO!**

# SECTION 1

# Understanding Nutrition and Testosterone


**CHAPTER 1**

Why the Meta-Test Boost Nutrition System? 10 Reasons This Is the Most Powerful Nutrition System for Men over 40

**CHAPTER 2**

Testosterone and Food – What You Must Know

**CHAPTER 3**

Nutrition 101 – Macronutrient Primer

**CHAPTER 4**

Calories and Testosterone

# CHAPTER 1

# Why the Meta-Test Boost Nutrition System?

## 10 Reasons This Is the Most Powerful Nutrition System for Men over 40

**MY META-TEST BOOST (MTB)** Nutrition System is specifically designed for guys like you who are over 40, 50, 60, and beyond.

I've done the research and used proven science to create a system that will help you naturally increase testosterone, balance your hormones, build lean muscle, and optimize your overall health.

So, buckle up, brother, because we're about to take on this nutrition game and win!

Let's take a look at the 10 reasons why my MTB Nutrition System is so powerful and why it's the perfect nutrition plan for men over the age of 40.

### 1. Supports Healthy Cholesterol Levels

I bet you didn't know your body needs cholesterol for hormone production, especially testosterone. It's true! And I know what you might be thinking – isn't cholesterol bad for your health?

Well, not all types of cholesterol are created equal. We're talking about HDL, or "good" cholesterol, which is essential for hormone synthesis and has a protective effect on your cardiovascular health.

It helps transport LDL ("bad") cholesterol and fats from your bloodstream and carries them to your liver. While low HDL has risks for cardiovascular health, high HDL cholesterol offers a protective effect [1]. (All science and research references for the "10 Reasons" presented here are listed at the end of this chapter.)

According to research, increasing your intake of good cholesterol is associated with greater muscle mass gain [2]. While many diets focus solely on reducing fat intake, the Meta-Test Boost Nutrition System recognizes the importance of healthy fats for testosterone production and overall health.

The plan emphasizes the consumption of foods such as eggs, beans and legumes, cold-water fatty fish, and olive oil, which are all rich in healthy fats.

By incorporating these foods into your diet, you can support healthy cholesterol levels, naturally increase testosterone levels, and achieve optimal health and fitness.

## 2. Supplies Healthy Starchy Complex Carbs for Energy and Hormones

Carbs have gotten a negative reputation due to the consumption of processed and refined carbohydrates, which can cause blood sugar imbalances, weight gain, and other health issues. But including healthy complex carbs every day in your diet is essential for brain health, energy, and thyroid function, the latter of which is responsible for controlling your metabolism.

Your thyroid gland plays a crucial role in regulating metabolism and energy levels. In other words, if you want to get rid of that belly fat and lose weight, you have to support your thyroid, so your body's metabolism will rev up and burn fat.

A 2014 study published in the journal *Nutrients* found that a diet rich in starchy complex carbohydrates can help support healthy thyroid function, which is important for regulating metabolism and energy levels [3]. The study also found that a diet high in complex carbs was associated with improved weight loss outcomes and increased fat oxidation, meaning that the body was better able to use stored fat as a source of energy.

Another study focusing on diet-hormone interactions found that the protein/carbohydrate ratio reciprocally alters the plasma levels of testosterone [4]. These findings suggest that complex carbs play an important role in overall health and weight loss and should not be avoided as part of a balanced diet.

If your current diet doesn't have enough starchy complex carbs to support thyroid function, your metabolic rate is going to slow, and you're going to start seeing all the symptoms of hypothyroidism – cold intolerance, fatigue, weight gain, muscle weakness and cramps, depression, and more.

Not to worry, the MTB Nutrition System focuses on a balanced plate that ensures you are eating enough starchy complex carbs, so you benefit from increased energy, fat loss, and better health.

### 3. Boosts Your Testosterone Levels

Building testosterone levels naturally is the backbone of the Meta-Test Boost Nutrition System. When you increase your intake of starchy complex carbohydrates, lean proteins, healthy fats, and vegetables/fruits (yes, these are a group of their own), you supply all the building blocks to naturally produce and increase your testosterone levels.

But specifically focusing on reducing cortisol levels is key to hormone balance.

Cortisol is a stress hormone. Although you need to release it throughout the day – like when you wake up, when you are training, or if you are in a fight-or-flight situation – when you have chronically high cortisol (generally caused by ongoing physical, mental, or emotional stress in your life) this actually causes an increase in chronic illness and kills your testosterone levels.

Both human and animal studies show that high circulating glucocorticoids (cortisol) have an inhibitory effect on testicular Leydig cell function, resulting in decreased testosterone production [5].

Simply put, cortisol is testosterone's kryptonite – the more cortisol constantly circulating in your body, the lower your testosterone levels will be.

So, to avoid increasing cortisol levels, my Meta-Test Boost Nutrition System includes foods to increase your intake of glucose from carbohydrates to support the release of the gonadotropin-releasing hormone, a "building block" of testosterone [6].

### 4. Reduces Your Estrogen Levels

When you hear the word *estrogen*, chances are you think about female hormones, right? Estrogen to women is like testosterone to men – but men need small amounts of estrogen for optimal function. Estradiol, the main form of estrogen, is important for male sexual function and modulates libido, erectile function, and spermatogenesis [7].

But here's the thing – too much estrogen will work against you.

When your estrogen levels are too high, it leads to decreased libido; an increase in belly fat storage, man boobs, risk of prostate cancer, cardiovascular disease, metabolic disorders; and a decrease in muscle mass and bone density. Worse, it kills your testosterone levels.

But obesity is another big concern for estrogen levels. High body fat levels increase aromatase activity, which converts testosterone to estradiol, resulting in decreased testosterone and elevated estrogen levels [8]. In turn, high estrogen levels further increase weight gain and fat storage, especially in the belly and breast tissue (man boobs).

In conjunction with weekly workouts to fight belly fat, the Meta-Test Boost Nutrition System focuses on eliminating foods with estrogenic activity to prevent high estrogen levels and increase testosterone levels.

### 5. Maximizes Muscle Growth

Sarcopenia is a natural loss of muscle mass due to aging, so once you reach the age of 40 your rate of losing muscle increases.

Some studies even estimate that up to 50 percent of your muscle mass can be lost by the time you reach your 80s [9].

Not only does a lack of muscle mass have enormous implications for your testosterone levels, but it also increases your risk of injury and affects your overall quality of life.

Although resistance training is one of the best ways to build muscle mass and strengthen bones to fight sarcopenia, you also need to consume sufficient protein to support muscle growth and protein synthesis.

Protein is the building block for your muscles, your bones, and the metabolic process that happens within your body. Because the body does not naturally produce protein, you need to consume it through high-quality protein foods. The Meta-Test Boost Nutrition System ensures you're meeting your protein goals with good-quality, lean proteins.

### 6. Supplies Bioavailable Protein for Hormone Synthesis

The second part of the protein equation is choosing the right kinds of protein.

I know what you're thinking: "Isn't protein, protein?"

Yes and no! Not all proteins are equal. I'm going to need to get a little "science" on you, so stick with me.

There are two kinds of proteins: complete and incomplete proteins.

Complete proteins contain all the essential amino acids necessary to build functional proteins. In general, all animal proteins are complete sources of protein.

On the other hand, incomplete proteins do not contain all essential amino acids in the appropriate ratios to build functional proteins; they are either missing essential amino acids entirely or don't have enough specific ones to stimulate muscle protein synthesis (MPS) and support hormone production.

The solution? The Meta-Test Boost Nutrition System focuses on helping you choose from a list of the highest quality animal proteins. Animal proteins tend to have a higher content of essential amino acids, which are the building blocks of protein and are crucial for muscle growth and repair.

Another factor to consider is the digestibility of proteins. Animal proteins are generally more easily digested and absorbed by the body. Ideally, you want to consume poultry (chicken, turkey, and duck), pasture-raised pork, grass-fed red meats (beef, venison, bison), eggs, and cold-water fatty fish, such as salmon. These foods are especially rich in healthy fats and zinc, which are needed to support testosterone production.

Now you may be saying, "Hey Funk, what about those plant proteins that vegans and vegetarians are praising so much?" Hitting your daily protein goals on a plant-based diet – and hitting the need for complete and bioavailable proteins – is extremely challenging.

Plant proteins are generally lower in one or more of the essential amino acids, which could limit their effectiveness in promoting muscle growth. Also, plant proteins are generally harder for your body to digest and absorb, which means they may be less bioavailable due to factors such as the presence of anti-nutrients or incomplete protein profiles.

One study published in *Nutrients* compared the effects of consuming equal amounts of protein from beef versus soy on muscle protein synthesis in young men. The researchers found that muscle protein synthesis was higher following consumption of the beef protein compared to soy protein [10a].

This being said, it is still possible to lose weight, balance hormones, and build muscle by combining your plant-based proteins with animal proteins and by consuming a sufficient amount of protein overall.

### 7. Loads Up on Micronutrients for Testosterone Production

So, eating enough macronutrients – proteins, healthy fats, starchy complex carbs, and veggies/fruits – is vital to support testosterone production, but what about vitamins and minerals?

The micronutrients are just as important as the macronutrients when it comes to fat loss, hormonal balance, and optimal health. Micronutrients are the vitamins and minerals that are in the foods you eat on the MTB Nutrition System.

To naturally increase testosterone levels, it's important you consume adequate amounts of essential vitamins and minerals. This includes zinc, magnesium, vitamin D, vitamin B6, vitamin K2, boron, and selenium, which all play crucial roles in testosterone production and overall health.

Zinc is essential for the production of testosterone and helps to regulate the hormone's activity in the body. Magnesium is also important for testosterone production, and a deficiency in this mineral has been linked to low testosterone levels in men.

Vitamin D is necessary for the body to produce testosterone, and a deficiency in this vitamin has been associated with lower levels of testosterone in men. Vitamin B6 helps to regulate testosterone levels and is important for the body's production of sex hormones. Vitamin K2 has been shown to increase testosterone levels and is important for overall health.

Boron has been shown to decrease the levels of sex hormone-binding globulin (SHBG), which binds to free testosterone in the blood and reduces its bioavailability. By reducing SHBG levels, boron can help increase the amount of free testosterone available for the body to use.

Finally, selenium is an essential mineral that has been shown to play a role in the production and regulation of thyroid hormones, which are important for the production of testosterone. It helps to reduce oxidative stress and inflammation in the body, which can, in turn, support healthy testosterone production.

### 8. Fights Estrogen with Fresh Foods

We discussed the importance of maintaining the proper balance of estrogen to testosterone before, but how do you counteract increases in estrogen aside from eliminating estrogenic foods?

By eating fresh foods!

The Meta-Test Boost Nutrition System puts a heavy focus on eating fruits and vegetables with every meal, especially antioxidant-rich berries and leafy greens. These are your best friends in fighting estrogen and boosting testosterone.

Cruciferous vegetables (broccoli, kale, cabbage, Brussels sprouts, cauliflower) rise to the top of this food category. They are great for reducing estrogen levels, because they contain a compound called 3,3'-Diindolylmethane, or DIM, that helps lower certain estrogens [10].

Through its effects on estrogen metabolism and inhibiting the aromatase enzyme, DIM can help support healthy testosterone levels by helping to maintain the appropriate level of free or active testosterone [11].

### 9. Boosts Hydration

"A gallon a day keeps the cortisol away." It's my favorite saying, and it's one of the best and simplest ways to reduce the risk of hormone imbalances. Why?

Dehydration is a huge factor that not only leads to impaired mental and physical performance, but it can also lead to reduced testosterone production.

How much water do you drink every day? Think about it . . .

Most men over 40 are chronically dehydrated, which plays a massive role in low testosterone. Whether you exercise regularly or not, dehydration directly influences cortisol levels, and this, in turn, influences your testosterone levels.

As you learned earlier, cortisol is the primary stress hormone produced by the adrenal glands in response to sympathetic activation (that is, stress). While cortisol is essential for many physiological functions, it acts as a natural testosterone suppressor when in excess.

A 2008 study published in the *Journal of Applied Physiology* looked at the effect of hydration state on the endocrine and metabolic responses to resistance exercise [12].

Seven healthy, resistance-trained men completed three identical resistance exercise bouts in various hydration states: euhydrated (optimal hydration), hypohydration (dehydration) by 2.5 percent body mass, and hypohydration by 5.0 percent body mass.

Results showed that hypohydration significantly increased levels of circulating concentrations of cortisol and norepinephrine, reduced the testosterone response to exercise, and altered carbohydrate and lipid metabolism.

What does this mean? The increase in testosterone levels normally associated with exercise is suppressed during a dehydrated state. So, even if you're exercising regularly at intensities sufficient to maximize the hormonal response to exercise, dehydration will blunt that response. But it's not just about drinking during training – you must stay hydrated all day. Failing to properly hydrate first thing in the morning can flatline your energy levels and fat burning for the entire day.

Ask yourself again – are you drinking enough?

In the Meta-Test Boost Nutrition System, ideally, you should drink at least half your body weight (in pounds) in ounces of water per day – or at least one gallon. For example, if you weigh 180 pounds, try to drink 90 ounces of water a day and, ideally, even more than that. (There are 128 fluid ounces in a gallon.)

If you're doing intense exercise and sweating like a beast or consuming caffeine (a diuretic), you want to increase your water intake to compensate.

### 10. It's Sustainable

How many times have you fallen for a fad diet that helps you lose weight, only to regain it the second you start eating "normally" again?

That's the thing with diets – they don't work.

So, think of the Meta-Test Boost Nutrition System as more of a *lifestyle*. Following this system, you will implement healthy eating practices to boost testosterone, lower estrogen, and build lean muscle.

And the best part? It's easy and sustainable.

There's no crazy carb cutting (I want you to eat carbs), no low-fat nonsense, and no starvation. It's about eating three balanced meals every day from a food list that literally appeals to everyone. If you don't have a taste for something, there are plenty of other options.

The Meta-Test Boost Nutrition System is a nutrition plan – a lifestyle – you can follow anywhere without worrying or sacrificing healthy living. It's simple, tasty, and insanely effective!

### Science and Research References for This Chapter

[1] Thirumalai A., Rubinow K. B., Page S. T. "An Update on Testosterone, HDL, and Cardiovascular Risk in Men." *Journal of Clinical Lipidology* 2015;10(3): 251-258.

[2] Riechman S. E., Andrews R. D., Maclean D. A., Sheather S. "Statins and Dietary and Serum Cholesterol Are Associated with Increased Lean Mass Following Resistance Training." *The Journals of Gerontology. Series A, Biological Sciences and Medical Sciences* 2007;62(10): 1164-1171.

[3] Medeiros-Neto G., Araujo R. L., Azevedo M. F., et al. "Nutritional Factors that Affect the Thyroid." In: Feingold K. R., Anawalt B., Boyce A., et al., editors. Endotext [Internet]. South Dartmouth (MA): MDText.com, Inc.; 2000-. Available from: https://www.ncbi.nlm.nih.gov/books/NBK285560/

[4] Anderson K. E., Rosner W., Khan M. S., et al. "Diet-Hormone Interactions: Protein/Carbohydrate Ratio Alters Reciprocally the Plasma Levels of Testosterone and Cortisol and Their Respective Binding Globulins in Man." *Life Sciences* 1987; 40(18): 1761-1768.

[5] Brownlee K. K., Moore A. W., Hackney A. C. "Relationship Between Circulating Cortisol and Testosterone: Influence of Physical Exercise." *Journal of Sports Science and Medicine* 2005;4(1): 76-83.

[6] Roland A. V., Moenter S. M. "Regulation of Gonadotropin-Releasing Hormone Neurons by Glucose." *Trends in Endocrinology and Metabolism* 2011;22(11):443-449.

[7] Schulster M., Bernie A. M., Ramasamy R. "The Role of Estradiol in Male Reproductive Function." *Asian Journal of Andrology* 2016;18(3): 435-440.

[8] Cohen P. G. "Obesity in Men: The Hypogonadal-Estrogen Receptor Relationship and Its Effect on Glucose Homeostasis." *Medical Hypotheses*. 2008;70(2):358-360.

[9] Walston J. D. "Sarcopenia in Older Adults." *Current Opinion in Rheumatology* 2012;24(6): 623-627.

[10a] Nutrients. 2019 Aug; 11(8): 1825.The Role of the Anabolic Properties of Plant- versus Animal-Based Protein Sources in Supporting Muscle Mass Maintenance: A Critical Review. Insaf Berrazaga,[1,2] Valérie Micard,[2] Marine Gueugneau,[1] and Stéphane Walrand[1,3,*]

[10] Lin T., Zirpoli G. R., McCann S. E., Moysich K. B., Ambrosone C.B., Tang L. "Trends in Cruciferous Vegetable Consumption and Associations with Breast Cancer Risk: A Case-Control Study." *Current Developments in Nutrition* 2017;1(8): e000448.

[11] Thomson C. A., Ho E., Strom M. B. "Chemopreventive Properties of 3,3'-Diindolylmethane in Breast Cancer: Evidence from Experimental and Human Studies." *Nutrition Reviews* 2016;74(7): 432-443.

[12] Judelson D. A., Maresh C. M., Yamamoto L. M., et al. "Effect of Hydration State on Resistance Exercise-Induced Endocrine Markers of Anabolism, Catabolism, and Metabolism." *Journal of Applied Physiology (1985)*. 2008;105(3): 816-824.

# CHAPTER 2

# Testosterone and Food – What You Must Know

**WE CAN DEFINE GOOD NUTRITION** as providing your body with the essential macronutrients, micronutrients, and water at the times you need them for optimal health and performance.

There's no denying the fact that what you eat has a huge influence on your body on a cellular level. By ensuring that you are eating the right foods, you ensure that you are always feeling your best.

Many people view nutrition as something that can help fight disease or that can help increase energy levels. And while it can certainly do both of those things, nutrition also impacts the hormone levels in your body.

Or, more specifically, your testosterone levels.

Testosterone is your dominant male sex hormone, and it plays a vital role in muscle growth, muscle size, muscle strength, muscle definition, athletic ability, aggression, fertility, libido, and metabolic rates as well as body composition.

*And that's just the tip of the iceberg in terms of its influence.*

As a man, if you want to maintain your energy, virility, and strength well into your golden years, then there is simply no other option but to prioritize increasing your testosterone levels. You don't want to miss out on all these benefits. You want your testosterone levels to be optimized to feel your best, look your best, and sustain optimal health.

The unfortunate fact is that when you reach the age of 30, your T-levels naturally decrease 1 to 2 percent every year. By the time you get into your 40s, your testosterone levels have completely dropped off.

Low testosterone levels can have a significant impact on a man's overall health and well-being, leading to a range of physical and psychological symptoms. Here are 15 common signs and symptoms of low testosterone that men should be aware of:

1. Low sex drive
2. Erectile dysfunction
3. Reduced muscle mass and strength
4. Increased body fat
5. Decreased bone density
6. Fatigue and low energy levels
7. Mood changes, including depression
8. Reduced motivation and drive
9. Memory and cognitive problems
10. Insomnia and poor sleep quality
11. Increased risk of cardiovascular disease
12. Higher risk of type 2 diabetes
13. Reduced body hair and beard growth
14. Weaker immune system
15. Infertility

The good news is that you can naturally increase your testosterone levels through living a healthy lifestyle that supports your nutrition and hormones. This is the biggest piece of the puzzle. This is where all this nutrition comes into play.

By taking steps now to prevent your testosterone levels from decreasing, you can ensure that you are setting yourself up for success down the road.

You may not even notice small decreases in your testosterone levels, but they can go unnoticed until the overall decrease is quite large. At that point, you finally figure out that you no longer feel like your previous self. It's easy to fall into the habit of feeling suboptimal and thinking it's your new normal – until one day you wake up and realize you just don't feel as healthy or energetic as you used to.

Everyone loses testosterone at a different rate, some faster than others, and it may take years before you start noticing the effects.

But don't wait until it's too late to take action, because, eventually, the effects will catch up to you.

## How Testosterone Works

In order to most effectively understand how nutrition is going to influence your testosterone levels, it's important that you take a second to understand testosterone production and the actions it has.

Testosterone production begins in the brain, not the testicles as many people may believe. There is a hormone called gonadotropin-releasing hormone (GnRH for short), and it travels to the pituitary gland. From there, GnRH stimulates the release of luteinizing hormone, which then travels through the blood all the way to the testes and activates certain enzymes that convert cholesterol into testosterone.

From this, you can now see the important role that cholesterol plays in testosterone production.

If you are not eating any cholesterol in your current diet, this can have a very negative influence on the results you see. This is why it's vitally important that you do not eliminate it entirely. Sure, you may lower your cholesterol levels to help boost your overall heart health, but you should not eliminate cholesterol.

In addition to influencing testosterone production in the first place, cholesterol may also influence testosterone production after the fact. After testosterone is produced, it will travel in the blood to the muscle cells and other tissues in the body either as *free testosterone* (also called *active testosterone*) or it will bind to a carrier protein and be called *bound testosterone*.

Only the free type of testosterone can work to increase muscle size, as this is the type that is able to enter the muscle cells. Bound testosterone essentially stays put; therefore, it's only acting on the tissue that it's bound to.

In some cases, the tissues such as body fat cells or brain tissues will convert testosterone into estrogen. This is one reason why we see heavier men who are overweight taking on more feminine-like qualities. Much of the testosterone they are producing is being converted into estrogen by their body's fat cells, thus they have a hormonal profile that leans more toward a female's rather than a male's hormonal profile.

This is a self-perpetuating cycle, because, as estrogen levels rise, this causes the man to gain more fat and a resulting lower and lower level of testosterone. Once you are on that bandwagon, it becomes challenging to get off.

By adjusting your diet in a manner that supports healthy testosterone production and a reduced estrogen production, you can get yourself on the right track. If you're currently very far off track, it may take you a little longer to get back on track again. With enough adherence to a proper nutrition plan, you will get there.

This testosterone-boosting plan consists of as many fresh and unprocessed foods as you can handle (there's just a bit of prep time) with ingredients you actually recognize and in amounts that are specific for your own body type.

It's time that you focus on eliminating the fake and processed "diet" convenience foods that so many people mistakenly believe are going to bring them maximum results. These include weight-loss packaged dinners, artificial sweeteners, "fat-free" foods that are laden with sugar, energy bars, and soy products as well as fake meats that are calorie controlled. In fact, you should avoid diet shakes as well, as often these contain unnatural ingredients that will simply not serve your body in the best manner possible.

The more you are putting these man-made foods into your body and the less you are focusing on foods that Mother Nature designed, the more these are going to adversely impact your hormones and internal biochemistry.

Usually when eating this unnatural food, you just wind up feeling addicted to it, gain weight, and, overall, you see your health go down.

The Meta-Test Boost Nutrition System is based on eating natural foods that offer you the highest overall concentrations of testosterone-boosting vitamins, minerals, and anti-inflammatory ingredients along with antioxidants and other nutrients such as phytochemicals.

These foods help you burn fat, build muscle, and keep you looking and feeling your best. They'll help keep you feeling younger while strengthening your immune system and fending off cancer. They also help you stabilize your mood while keeping your heart healthy and your breathing regulated. You'll find that you sleep better when eating these foods and sleep deeper as well.

So, with that said, let's begin diving into the program and give you the details you need to know about each of the macronutrients.

## CHAPTER 3

# Nutrition 101 – Macronutrient Primer

**IN YOUR DIET, YOU'LL ENCOUNTER** three main types of nutrients, known as *macronutrients*: proteins, dietary fats, and carbohydrates. They're classified as macronutrients, because we consume them in large amounts, and they provide calories for energy. On the other hand, you have micronutrients, such as vitamins and minerals, which are only required in small amounts and do not contain calories. I'll address micronutrients in a later chapter.

Each macronutrient has a specific role in the body, and it's crucial to have all three in your diet. Let's dive into the unique functions of each, so you can better understand how they work together to support your health and fitness goals.

### Proteins

Chances are, you've heard of protein before. Protein is the macronutrient that most bodybuilders think they need in abundance to build muscle. Most think they need more protein than they actually do, and they tend to overload on it at the expense of the other two macronutrients.

Protein is a critical macronutrient and is key for building lean muscle tissue. It supplies the amino acids that your muscle tissues are made from, so without these amino acids you won't have much success in building muscle.

You can't build muscle out of thin air, so amino acids are critical. In addition to providing the building blocks that muscle is made of, amino acids are also key for creating neurotransmitters in the body, which are essentially chemical messenger signals. Neurotransmitters help ensure everything in your body is functioning in a coordinated manner.

If you don't get enough protein it can hinder testosterone development. However, if you get too much protein it can also have similar effects. The most common recommendation is 1.5 grams of protein per kilogram of body weight per day or 0.7 grams of protein per pound of body weight per day.

As some protein will likely be used as a fuel source, this means you need more protein, so enough is left over to complete all the key roles that protein needs to carry out. This ensures you will always be getting a sufficient amount.

If you want to go by percentages, then getting around 20 to 25 percent of your total daily calorie intake from protein is recommended. For example, if you take in 2,000 calories a day, plan to eat 400 to 500 calories of protein every day.

Keep in mind that protein is the hardest nutrient of all to break down and digest, so if you are consuming too much, this will place extra strain on the body. As a result, your cortisol levels may increase, and if this takes place, then you are likely to see a reduction in testosterone as a result.

Of all three macronutrients – proteins, carbohydrates, and dietary fats – protein may be the most important for building lean muscle, but it's the least important for keeping your testosterone levels elevated.

So, focus on the fine line between enough protein but not too much.

It should also be noted that vegetarian sources of protein (from vegetables, whole grains, and soy-based foods) are not as beneficial for keeping testosterone levels higher compared to meat sources of protein.

One study published in the *British Journal of Nutrition* noted that when test subjects got the majority of their protein from meat versus tofu for a period of 4 weeks, the meat eaters had 10 percent higher overall testosterone levels (1).

So, really do try to focus your protein intake as much as possible on lean meat sources. This includes foods like organic chicken and turkey, free-range beef, free-range whole eggs, and wild-caught salmon and other fish and seafood.

When consuming beef protein, you want to aim for grass-fed whenever possible, as this will have the best overall amino acid profile for testosterone boosting coupled with favorable types of dietary fats.

## The Facts on Dietary Fats

While many people are under the impression that fats are to be feared as far as maintaining an optimal body composition goes, this is not the case at all. In fact, you need dietary fat in order for your body to produce testosterone.

Remember how we noted the role that cholesterol plays in the body when it comes to producing testosterone? Well, you get cholesterol from dietary fat. Without fat, there is no testosterone, and without testosterone there is no lean muscle mass tissue.

Dietary fat is critical for the development of steroid hormones. This makes sense, because the backbone of those steroid hormones is a substance called gonane, which is a 17-carbon fat molecule.

Research (2) has also indicated that men who consume a high-fiber, low-fat diet tend to have levels of testosterone lower than that of men who consume a lower-fiber, higher-fat diet. This doesn't mean you should banish all vegetables from your diet plan and only eat nuts, seeds, and oils, but it does mean that moderation is key.

You don't want to eat too many vegetables in your diet at the expense of dietary fat, or you may pay the price of doing so. This is particularly notable for men who are trying to lose weight, as vegetable intake usually goes up among dieting individuals, because vegetables are such a low-calorie food.

Not all fat is created equal, however, and certain fats have a much more positive influence on testosterone levels than other fats do.

There are four main types of dietary fats to know about: trans fats, polyunsaturated fatty acids (PUFA), monounsaturated fatty acids (MUFA), and saturated fatty acids (SFA).

### *Trans Fats*

Trans fats are a man-made type of fat that happens when vegetable oil is hydrogenated. You want to avoid this type of fat at all costs, as it has no real benefits for the body and can put you at risk for a wide number of diseases. It can also lower testosterone production.

### *Polyunsaturated Fats (PUFA)*

Polyunsaturated fats, or PUFA, are often regarded as healthy sources of fat. However, if consumed in large quantities, they can lower testosterone output. This type of fat makes up a large quantity of our intake of omega-6 fatty acids.

While you do need some omega-6 fatty acids on a regular basis, taking in too many will lead to greater levels of inflammation, as it's not balanced with the levels of omega-3 fatty acids you're consuming. Examples of these types of foods include sunflower seeds, flaxseeds, flax oil, corn oil, soybean oil, and safflower oil.

The one exception to the rule is omega-3 fatty acids. You do want to get these in your diet on a regular basis, despite being a PUFA, as these fats will lower inflammation levels in the body, support good health, and should have no negative influence on testosterone function. Examples of these types of food include cold-water fatty fish such as salmon, mackerel, tuna, herring, and sardines and various nuts and seeds including walnuts and chia seeds.

It's the balance between omega-6 fatty acids and omega-3 fatty acids that you should be striving to optimize. Sadly, most people in today's world take in far more omega-6 fatty acids than they do omega-3 fatty acids.

### *Monounsaturated Fats (MUFA)*

Next, you have the monounsaturated fats, or MUFA, as they are often called. These types of fatty acids have only one double bonded carbon-carbon atom in their structure, while the remaining bonds are single.

This makes them more stable than PUFA and less prone to oxidation that can cause fatty acids to become harmful.

We are seeing some research (3) that suggests those who have higher intakes of MUFA in their diet may show elevated levels of testosterone. Therefore, this is something that you do want to take into account.

Examples of these foods include olive oil, avocados, salmon, olives, and peanut oil.

### *Saturated Fats*

The last type of fat you need to be aware of is saturated fatty acids. As you likely already know, saturated fat has quite a bad rap, as many people believe it is a leading contributor to heart disease.

And it is, in fact, going to be linked to higher levels of heart disease if you consume it in large quantities from unnatural sources (think deep-fried foods, ice creams, fast food, and so forth). If you are getting saturated fat from wholesome sources such as steak, eggs, and dairy, then you need not worry. In fact, this saturated fat can help boost testosterone and even protect your heart health by doing so.

Saturated fat is, as we spoke about earlier, necessary for the manufacture of testosterone, so without it you won't get very far. The main thing you need to focus on with your intake of saturated fat is where you are getting that fat from, as this will make all the difference.

Saturated fat is found in foods like beef, pork, eggs, dairy products, and butter.

Men who are looking to boost their testosterone levels can safely eat up to 30 to 50 percent of their total dietary fat intake from saturated fat, with the remaining coming primarily from monounsaturated fatty acids, while minimizing the amount of polyunsaturated fatty acids they consume.

In general, of your overall diet, you can safely get around 25 to 40 percent of your total calorie intake from dietary fats, depending on your goals and how many calories you are consuming.

Keep in mind, the more carbohydrates you eat, the less total percentage of dietary fats will be in your diet and vice versa. Those who are trying to burn fat and lose weight (thus taking in fewer calories from fat sources) will notice fats make up a smaller portion of their diet plan, while those who are building muscle may notice it is slightly higher.

## Carbohydrates

Finally, the last macronutrient that we need to discuss is carbohydrates.

Just like dietary fats, many people are starting to believe that carbohydrates are also poor choices with regard to maintaining a lowered body weight. We are seeing people everywhere begin cutting their carbohydrates way back in an effort to melt fat and burn off the "spare tire" they've accumulated.

The issue is, first, carbohydrates are the primary source of fuel for the muscles as well as the brain.

The first thing you will likely notice when you begin cutting back your carbohydrate intake is that your gym performance will begin to dramatically decline. Your body will feel sluggish and slow, and your strength will be reduced. This is all because you just don't have the carbohydrates available to push through those heavy sets and give your muscles the power they need.

Next, although cutting carbs can be tempting when trying to lose weight, it will actually cause your body to go into starvation mode. Your body needs carbohydrates for energy, and if it doesn't get enough, it will slow down to conserve energy.

This will lead to a slowdown of your metabolism, making it harder to burn fat and lose weight. In addition, cutting carbs can also lead to low energy levels and brain fog, making it difficult to focus and get things done. It's important to find a balance with your carb intake to ensure you have the energy you need while still reaching your weight loss goals.

Finally, carbohydrates are closely connected to testosterone production as well.

If your carbohydrate intake is too low, the body will start to perceive an energy shortage is taking place (a famine) and will begin to slow down or stop many of the unnecessary functions that aren't needed for survival. In women, we often see a disruption of the menstrual cycle when this takes place, and in males, we see a dip in testosterone levels.

Likewise, when your carbohydrate intake begins to dip significantly, this can shut down thyroid production as well, so you may notice a slowing in the metabolic rate.

So, cutting back on carbs is not even that beneficial as far as fat loss goes either.

What's more important than how many carbohydrates you eat (within reason of course, since your total calorie intake still needs to be in check) is where you are getting those carbohydrates from.

If you are feasting on processed sources of carbohydrates each and every day – like donuts, sugary cereals, and white pasta – there's no doubt this is not going to be great news for your health or body composition.

If you are feasting on quality sources of nutrient-dense carbohydrates, on the other hand, this is a completely different story. These carbohydrates will release their energy slowly, keeping your blood glucose levels balanced.

There are two main types of carbohydrates. Let's look at each type briefly and what it will do for you.

### *Complex Carbohydrates (Good Carbs)*

The first type is complex carbohydrates, and it is the variety that you want to focus on. This type of carbohydrate is harder to break down by the body, so it won't produce a rapid release of glucose into the bloodstream, spiking your levels and causing a temporary "high" before you crash.

There are high-energy complex carbohydrates and fibrous complex carbohydrates. High-energy complex carbohydrates are your whole grains. This includes white rice, quinoa, barley, steel-cut oats, and Ezekiel bread. Starchy vegetables such as sweet potatoes, squash, and pumpkin also fit into this list, so keep those in mind as well.

As you progress through this book, you'll see that I refer to all good carbs as *starchy complex carbohydrates* – this includes both the whole grains and starchy vegetables mentioned above. These carbohydrates should provide a large portion of your diet when trying to build muscle; cut back on them slightly when dieting. These are going to have a great influence on testosterone levels.

Then there are fibrous carbohydrates as well. These carbohydrates are vegetables and are rich in dietary fiber while being low in calories. You want to keep these present in your diet. As you'll see when we talk more specifically about the Meta-Test Boost Nutrition System, I encourage you to eat a healthy portion of vegetables and fruits with every meal, because they are packed with micronutrients.

As I noted earlier, taking in too much dietary fiber, especially coupled with a reduced fat intake, can cause a decline in testosterone levels. Vegetables are exceptionally nutrient dense, however, so you should not remove them from the diet, or you will miss out on many of the benefits they have to offer.

Complex carbohydrates are ideal to eat before and after your workout sessions, as it's at this point in the day they will help provide you with the greatest energy and benefits.

Fruit is slightly unique in that it typically contains a mixture of fruit sugars and fiber.

Now, as I'll discuss in a second, you typically want to stay away from sugar as often as you can. Fruit sugar, however, is the exception.

While you still shouldn't overload on it, it's handled by the body differently than regular sugar, because it's composed of a mixture of fructose and glucose. Only the glucose will spike blood glucose levels, therefore, this type of sugar can be less problematic. Fruit is also relatively low in calories and packed full of antioxidants, so it's amazing for you for overall health benefits.

Research illustrates just how important a good carbohydrate intake is as well. A research study that was published in the *European Journal of Applied Physiology* (4) had men consume a high-carb diet during intense training and then also had another group consume a lower-carb diet during the same training. After the trial period ended, it was indicated that men who consumed the higher-carb diet showed significantly better overall testosterone levels than men who consumed the lower-carb diet.

I recommend getting about 40 to 50 percent of your total daily calorie intake from starchy complex carbohydrates.

### *Simple Carbohydrates (Bad Carbs)*

Next, we have simple carbohydrates. You want to avoid these carbohydrate sources, since they will quickly reduce testosterone levels, causing issues for your health and fitness goals.

Simple sugars are also going to overwork your pancreas, forcing it to pump out excess insulin all the time. If this goes on for lengthy periods of time, diabetes can result. Simple carbohydrates are also typically very low in nutrients, as they are heavily processed so, again, are not optimal for anyone's diet. It's recommended to stay clear of these foods whenever possible.

Examples of simple carbohydrates include:

- Cookies
- Crackers
- Granola bars
- Sugary cereals
- White bread

- Donuts
- Baked goods
- White pasta
- Cakes
- Muffins
- Cupcakes
- Any other processed foods

The more you can cut these foods out of your diet, the better off you're going to be.

In addition to bad carbs, the foods in this list also deliver a dose of gluten. Gluten tends to be a particular offender for many people, as they have an insensitivity to it. Gluten can lead to inflammation, aches and pains, high cortisol levels, and even suppressed testosterone in time.

So, what's the takeaway from this?

## STAY AWAY!

Focus on eating wholesome carbohydrates that come straight from the ground naturally rather than eating carbohydrates that have been man made. If you follow this simple principle, you will set yourself up for success.

## CHAPTER 4

# Calories and Testosterone

**BEFORE WE MOVE ON,** it's important to quickly discuss calories. The first important thing you must note is that not all three macronutrients contain the same number of calories.

Most carbohydrates and protein contain four calories per gram, while dietary fats contain nine calories per gram. As such, it's vital to understand that if you eat too many fat-rich foods, the calories will add up quickly, and you will gain weight.

This means you simply need to monitor how many grams of fat you are eating each day to hit your targets.

In addition, you need to check your overall calorie intake. For testosterone optimization, it's best to be at your current maintenance calorie intake or even slightly above. This is going to help favor the anabolic hormone release and help reduce any chance of cortisol making an appearance.

If you cannot be at a maintenance calorie level because you are trying to lose weight, then use a small calorie deficit. You should not go more than about 300 to 500 calories below maintenance. A crash diet (defined as a diet plan that has you taking in dramatically reduced calories) is not going to do your testosterone levels any favors.

## Daily Intake for Maximum Testosterone Production

So, to summarize, what should you aim for when on a diet to boost testosterone levels?

Your calorie level should be divided up, so you are consuming around:

- 20 to 25 percent total dietary protein intake
- 25 to 40 percent total dietary fat intake
- 40 to 50 percent total carbohydrate intake

If you can get your numbers lined up so you are hitting each of these targets, you should feel quite confident that you are on track to seeing great results.

Finally, if you're wondering how to count calories and figure out percentages of macronutrients for your real-life diet plan, don't worry! Keep reading, brother. I've got you covered.

## SECTION 2

# Optimizing Nutrition for Testosterone Production

**CHAPTER 5**

Testosterone-Boosting Superfoods

**CHAPTER 6**

The Power Micronutrients for Optimal Testosterone Production

**CHAPTER 7**

How Hydration Factors into Your Overall Health

**CHAPTER 8**

Foods That Are Crushing Your Testosterone Levels

# CHAPTER 5
# Testosterone-Boosting Superfoods

**BEFORE WE GO TO THE NEXT TOPIC,** I want to speak a little about the superfoods that will help really kick-start your testosterone levels into high gear.

These foods are going to help really improve your health and put you in a favorable position for greater overall testosterone release. Think of these as extra-special foods that, if you can get them into your plan, you'll really benefit from them more than other foods out there.

## Coconut Oil

Coconut oil is a great source of medium chain triglycerides, which are important for providing immediate energy to the body, stabilizing blood glucose levels, boosting your immune system, and helping to increase your metabolic rate. Including this food in your diet can help you preserve your testosterone levels.

## Raw Nut Butter

Nut butter is another great source of healthy monounsaturated fats, so it is good for helping to maintain proper testosterone levels. Whether you choose cashew butter, almond butter, or walnut butter, these nut butters can be good to consume in moderation. Note that you only want the natural variations, however, as processed nut butters tend to contain more of the polyunsaturated fats you don't want and also are higher in sugar.

### Brazil Nuts

What's unique about Brazil nuts? This superfood is ideal to eat for those who are looking to boost their testosterone levels, because they are a rich source of selenium, which is a powerful booster. They also don't contain quite as many fats as other nuts, so they can help you keep your fat intake to a reasonable level.

### Extra Virgin Olive Oil

When preparing salad dressings, you can't go wrong with extra virgin olive oil. While you should not heat this oil to high temperatures, it's great for non-heat or low-heat cooking and is perfect for offering the right dietary fat ratio to complement testosterone enhancement.

Studies (5) indicate that men who replace some of their fat intake with extra virgin olive oil note a 17.4 percent increase in testosterone levels.

### Avocados

Another great food to consume to help keep your healthy fat intake where it needs to be is the avocado. Avocados contain 10 grams of fat per half avocado serving, and the majority of this fat comes from monounsaturated fat sources.

### Grass-Fed Butter

Many people fear butter, but grass-fed butter is actually one of the best foods you can consume as far as your fat intake is concerned. It contains an excellent source of natural saturated fats, which will encourage peak testosterone production. It's also a much heart-healthier form of fat than margarine.

### Sweet Potatoes

One of the best carbohydrate sources you should look into are sweet potatoes. Despite their "sweet" name, sweet potatoes don't actually contain much sugar, and the sugar they do contain will help stabilize your testosterone levels instead of causing a boost and a crash like sugars from processed foods.

Sweet potatoes also help elevate the levels of adiponectin, which helps to mobilize fat in the body, so these could be a good fat-burning food if you need to shed a bit of excess body fat for optimal testosterone production.

The body tends to better absorb the nutrients found in sweet potatoes when some dietary fat is present, so try placing some grass-fed butter on them for a delicious side dish that works with any meal.

### Beets

Consider consuming beets on a regular basis. They're lower in carbohydrates than some other foods, so they can help you keep your total calorie intake in check. More importantly, they contain nitrates and betaine, which can help your liver to chelate estrogen out of your body.

Remember that estrogen counteracts testosterone, so the more you have present, the less likely you are to have higher testosterone levels. It's vital to minimize estrogen whenever you can.

### Black Beans

Black beans also rank high on the list of superfoods to eat if you hope to boost your testosterone levels. The reason? They are a rich source of zinc, which is closely associated with testosterone production. More on this to come, but for now know that men who are low in zinc intake often also have lower-than-average testosterone production.

Just keep beans to moderate serving sizes, as they are also high in dietary fiber. But do get them in!

### Pumpkin Seeds

Another food rich in zinc? Pumpkin seeds. These are excellent for boosting testosterone production and will also provide you with a good dose of healthy fats. You can easily eat them on their own or serve them with a meal as a topping.

### White Button Mushrooms

On the vegetable side of things, make sure you incorporate white button mushrooms into your meals. (I know what you're thinking: "Hey Funk, mushrooms aren't vegetables!" Nutrition science places mushrooms in the vegetable category.)

### Spinach

Next on the list of superfoods is spinach. Spinach is a fantastic source of magnesium, which is important for building muscle and maintaining a proper functioning reproductive system, including adequate testosterone levels.

When it comes to leafy greens, many people think kale is the best superfood. However, kale isn't nearly as high in magnesium as spinach. So, if testosterone boosting is your goal, opt for spinach instead of kale.

### Broccoli

Next up, we have broccoli. This is a favorite vegetable for many, because it's quite versatile and easy to cook. If you've been in the bodybuilding world for a while, chances are you've had your fair share of broccoli. If you've been eating broccoli, this is great news, because broccoli contains indoles – compounds that are necessary for flushing estrogen out of the body. Remember, too much estrogen will wreak havoc on testosterone, so the more you can diminish the presence of estrogen, the better.

As estrogen levels tend to increase with age, older men in particular will want to get in as much broccoli as they can. This will help counteract the rise in estrogen that typically takes place with age.

### Eggs

Eggs are another food that many men fear, thinking it will do them no good to eat and will only raise their cholesterol levels. Really, sugar is what dramatically raises cholesterol levels. Eggs, despite the cholesterol they contain, won't cause concern for heart health as long as you are consuming moderate amounts.

What's more, the cholesterol found in eggs is what your body needs to maintain optimized testosterone levels, so you definitely do not want to cut them out.

### Wild-Caught Salmon

Wild-caught salmon is next on the list of delicious foods to eat to help boost testosterone. The primary benefit of this fish variety is the strong profile of omega-3 fatty acids it provides; most people are not getting enough of these healthy fatty acids in their diet plans.

You really do want to opt for wild-caught salmon, though, not farm raised. Farm-raised salmon contains less than 25 percent of the vitamin content that wild-caught salmon contains and won't provide as much of the beneficial omega-3 fatty acids. You want to aim to eat salmon at least two to three times per week, if possible.

### Yellow Fin Tuna

Tuna is another fish variety to consider adding to your meal plan. The nice thing about tuna is that it's also rich in selenium, which is one of the best testosterone boosters out there. It will also provide you with a strong dose of vitamin D as well as omega-3 fatty acids. As far as protein sources go, it's a terrific option.

### Grass-Fed Bison

Finally, don't overlook grass-fed bison. This form of protein is leaner than steak but still provides a solid dose of zinc and vitamin B12, both of which are important for testosterone support.

While it's definitely a good idea to include some beef (steak) in your diet plan, you do want to consume it in moderation. Bison is an excellent fill-in for those other times.

So, there you have the top superfoods that you should focus on eating whenever you can as you get started on the Meta-Test Boost Nutrition System. All of these will provide your body with the support you need to get your critical male hormone – testosterone – to the level you want it to be.

## CHAPTER 6

# The Power Micronutrients for Optimal Testosterone Production

**WHEN IT COMES TO BOOSTING** your testosterone levels, it's not just about the macronutrients. Micronutrients, such as vitamins and minerals, play a crucial role in testosterone production and overall health.

For example, zinc is an essential mineral for the production of testosterone. Studies have shown that men with zinc deficiencies have lower testosterone levels than those who consume enough of this micronutrient. Other micronutrients, such as vitamin D, vitamin B, and magnesium, have also been shown to have a positive impact on testosterone levels.

In addition to boosting testosterone, consuming a wide range of micronutrients can help improve your overall health and well-being. Many micronutrients act as antioxidants, protecting your cells from damage and reducing inflammation throughout the body.

To ensure you're getting enough micronutrients to support testosterone production, it's important to eat a varied and balanced diet that includes a wide range of fruits, vegetables, and whole foods. You may also consider taking a high-quality multivitamin or mineral supplement to fill in any nutritional gaps in your diet.

Remember, when it comes to boosting your testosterone levels, every little bit counts, which is why I focus on both micronutrients and macronutrients when choosing the foods for the Meta-Test Boost Nutrition System.

Let's look at some of the most important micronutrients that can help you boost your testosterone levels.

## Zinc

Zinc is one mineral that is essential for optimal testosterone. As we noted earlier, men who do not have adequate zinc levels often show signs of testosterone deficiency, as was noted by study published in the *Nutrition Journal* (6).

As a man, you lose a large amount of zinc each time you ejaculate, so the more active your sex life is, the more at-risk you are of deficiency of this mineral.

In addition to supporting testosterone production, zinc is also imperative for keeping your immune system healthy and strong, for healing wounds, and for helping with protein synthesis and cell division.

You should aim for 40 mg of zinc per day, and don't go too much above this or it will interfere with your ability to absorb other minerals. Some people think it's a more-is-better situation, but this is not the case. The best way to take in more zinc is through your diet, so focus on zinc-rich foods over supplements when possible.

The best sources of zinc include grass-fed beef, oysters, crab and lobster, meat and poultry, legumes, pumpkin seeds, as well as nuts and other seeds.

## Vitamin D

Next on our list of power micronutrients is vitamin D. Vitamin D, often called the *sunshine vitamin*, is an important micronutrient that often gets forgotten. It works in conjunction with calcium to promote stronger bones and help prevent the risk of osteoporosis.

Vitamin D is also vital for helping to ensure adequate testosterone, as noted by a study published in the *Hormone and Metabolic Research* journal (7), a healthy libido, as well as sperm production. If you don't spend much time outside in the sun, chances are you are low in vitamin D levels, because it's not found in many of the foods we eat on an everyday basis.

This is why supplementation with this vitamin is typically key. You want to aim for

4,000 IUs per day for optimal testosterone support. Keep in mind that this is a fat-soluble vitamin, so again, more is not better. If you take in too much, it'll get stored in the body's fat cells and could lead to toxicity.

You will find vitamin D in vitamin D-fortified orange juice and milk, salmon bones (if you consume them), and egg yolks. So, there are a few places where you can get it in your diet. However, generally speaking, these foods won't provide sufficient amounts of vitamin D to meet your needs. If you are choosing salmon and eggs to help meet your daily quota, choosing wild-caught salmon and free-range eggs will definitely help. However, it's still advisable to look into a supplement as well.

## Selenium

Selenium is next on the list of minerals to focus on if you hope to take your testosterone to the next level. This mineral is found in the soil and, in food, is found primarily in lean meats and fish. It's an important part of the equation for keeping your metabolism in proper working order, and it promotes higher testosterone levels thanks to its glutathione stimulating effects.

You should aim to take in approximately 400 mcg of selenium daily. Some of the best sources of selenium are Brazil nuts, yellow fin tuna, halibut, sardines, grass-fed beef, and turkey. For instance, a four-ounce serving of yellow fin tuna will provide you with 200 percent of your total selenium intake. Tuna is also an excellent source of vitamin D, omega fatty acids, and protein, so it's a smart addition to your testosterone-boosting diet plan.

## Vitamin A

You also want to make sure you are getting enough vitamin A. This fat-soluble vitamin is stored in the testes, along with a few other places in the body, and studies have demonstrated that when no active form of vitamin A is present in the body, testosterone levels begin to drop off rapidly. As this happens, estrogen levels begin to rise, which just worsens the situation.

Interestingly, in prepubertal teens, those who take a vitamin A supplement combined with an iron supplement note that they have early onset of puberty, indicating just how powerful these nutrients can be.

The best sources of vitamin A include winter and butternut squash, sweet potatoes, kale, carrots, beef liver, spinach, dried apricots, broccoli, butter, and egg yolks.

## Magnesium

The next mineral you'll want to focus on in order to achieve the best possible overall level of testosterone is magnesium. This mineral plays a critical role in keeping your muscle contractions and nerve signals regular, promoting a strong immune system, and regulating the heartbeat. It works in conjunction with calcium and vitamin D to help promote better bone health. Finally, it helps stimulate your natural release of testosterone.

The best sources of magnesium in the diet are bananas, beans, kale, almonds, dark chocolate, and yogurt. Bananas especially make for a great pre- or post-workout boost, so I'd highly recommend having one of these each and every day.

## Vitamin C

Most people think of vitamin C as the main vitamin you take when you feel a cold coming on, but it's important for far more than that. While it's true that vitamin C will strengthen your immune system and help give you that boost when you need it, vitamin C is also key for helping to ward off oxidative damage, as it acts as a powerful antioxidant in the body.

Vitamin C also has a protective effect on testosterone molecules because of its ability to counteract some of the effects of cortisol.

Vitamin C is fairly easy to get into your diet simply by eating a wide variety of fresh fruits and vegetables. Some of the key sources include guava, black currants, red peppers, kiwi, green peppers, oranges, strawberries, papaya, and broccoli.

As long as you are focusing on eating a variety of fresh fruits and vegetables, you'll be able to get this power micronutrient in your diet plan.

## Calcium

Calcium is an important nutrient to take in regardless of what it does for your testosterone levels simply because it helps foster stronger bone growth.

If you start to suffer from weak and brittle bones, this will really play a hindering role in your ability to lift heavy weights in the gym – or lift any weight at all. So, if that happens, you will really see a detriment in your progress.

Calcium is important for controlling the neurotransmitter release that takes place between cells and hormones, including testosterone. Research (8) suggests that calcium can help elevate testosterone levels post-exercise, which is critical, because this is when you want your levels to be highest. Then it can be used to help with the signaling of more muscle building.

The best sources of calcium to consume include milk, plain yogurt, hard cheeses, grass-fed whey protein powder, almonds, sardines, seeds, and lentils.

## Boron

Finally, boron is one mineral you may never hear talked about but should be discussed as well. Scientists have noted in the journal *Nutrition Research* (9) that this particular mineral may help boost testosterone levels by a significant amount (up to 29 percent) upon supplementation, so it's worth looking into.

You will need to take in above 6 mg of this mineral in order to see these kinds of results, so it's not something that you'll likely be able to achieve with food alone. Supplementation will likely be key.

The best food sources of this mineral are chickpeas, almonds, beans, vegetables, bananas, walnuts, and avocados. Eating these regularly and combining them with a supplement will be your best option.

So, there you have a closer look at the key vitamins and minerals that you'll want to focus on taking in if you are going to see optimal health.

Now let's look at the second critical element to be considered – hydration.

# CHAPTER 7
# How Hydration Factors into Your Overall Health

**MANY PEOPLE OVERLOOK** the influence that proper hydration can have on their health, their physical performance, and their hormonal levels. We put a lot of attention into the foods we are eating, but when it comes to what we are drinking, we tend to fall short.

Hydration is critical. Think about it this way: Your body can only survive for days without water. But you can go weeks, if not months, without food.

So, which do you think is more essential to proper functioning? The answer should be clear. Even slight levels of dehydration can have a large influence on how well you feel.

Most people today are filling their fluid needs with coffee, colas, and alcohol, all of which contain caffeine and serve as a diuretic. This does not hydrate you adequately, and often these beverages pose serious drawbacks due to the calories they contain and lack of micronutrients.

Ask yourself this question: When was the last time you had a glass of pure water? You may not even have had one today. We're all so focused on serving ourselves things that please our taste buds, and since water has virtually no taste, it often gets left behind.

Some of the key effects of dehydration include:

- Increased thirst
- Dry mouth
- Feeling lethargic or more tired than normal
- Showing lowered urine output
- Suffering from headaches
- Dry skin
- Dizziness
- Lowered endurance levels
- Lowered strength levels
- Poor recovery
- Lowered blood pressure levels
- Rapid heart rates
- Suffering from a high fever
- Poor skin elasticity
- Seizures (when the case is severe enough)

Dehydration impacts every cell in your body, so you can rest assured it will not go unnoticed in the Meta-Test Boost Nutrition System.

In terms of your hormonal output, one way that dehydration influences you is through the production of cortisol. When you are in a dehydrated state and perform physical activity, you have a greater chance of suffering from higher cortisol levels after this activity, which in turn counteracts the release of testosterone.

Cortisol is the enemy when trying to build a healthy, great-looking body, so you really want to do everything you can to avoid it.

Exercising itself tends to increase testosterone release, but when you are exercising in a dehydrated state, this is another story. Dehydration tends to mask the testosterone elevation you should be seeing, and, as a result, you notice a downward trend in your testosterone levels.

On top of that, dehydration also influences the production of growth hormones.

Human growth hormone (HGH) is a natural hormone that is produced by the pituitary gland, which is located right behind the bridge of the nose. This hormone is responsible for the development and growth of children as they enter their puberty years. As adults, HGH is important for reducing the signs of aging, improving muscle strength, accelerating the recovery rate from injuries, and improving weight-loss results, and it can even help assist those who are suffering from erectile dysfunction.

As you grow older, levels of both HGH and testosterone naturally tend to decline, so it's up to you to implement lifestyle changes that will help maximize your levels.

One of the ways to optimize HGH is through adequate hydration. Research (10) shows that those who are in a dehydrated state show lower overall exercise-induced pulses of growth hormone release, thus their overall daily levels will be lower.

Exercise can be a powerful influencer of growth hormone release, but if you aren't drinking enough water, you'll lose out on these benefits.

For the best results with your hydration plan, you want to focus on drinking strictly water whenever possible. Other good options are sparkling water (which is free of sugar and artificial sweetener), grass-fed whey protein shakes, herbal teas, and black decaf coffee. If you can focus on drinking a sufficient quantity of these beverages in your diet plan, you'll be hydrating yourself well.

How much water should you drink? Remember my favorite saying, which I mentioned in Chapter 1: "A gallon a day keeps the cortisol away." In that chapter I explained that, ideally, you should drink at least half your body weight (in pounds) in ounces of water per day – or at least one gallon.

Remember, drinking water is one of the best and simplest ways you can reduce the risk of hormone imbalances.

## CHAPTER 8

# Foods That Are Crushing Your Testosterone Levels

**OKAY, BY NOW I HOPE** you are learning about the power of foods and how they significantly impact your health, fat loss, muscle growth, and testosterone levels.

Unfortunately, certain foods can harm your testosterone production, even if you're doing everything else right.

In this chapter, I'll go over the worst offenders first, so you can be aware of what to avoid. I will also include a full list of more foods to stay away from, especially if you are trying to get back into shape. Here's an overview of the four worst offenders, and I'll dive into details later in this chapter.

First, let's talk about soy. Soy products, including soy milk, tofu, and edamame, contain high levels of phytoestrogens. These compounds mimic the effects of estrogen in the body, which can decrease testosterone levels, especially when consumed in large amounts.

Next on the list is sugar. High sugar intake is linked to insulin resistance, which can disrupt hormone levels, including testosterone. Plus, sugar is high in calories, which can contribute to weight gain, another factor that can negatively impact testosterone production.

Alcohol is another major culprit. Excessive alcohol consumption can lead to liver damage, which in turn impairs testosterone synthesis. Plus, alcohol is known to increase estrogen levels, further hampering testosterone production.

Finally, let's talk about processed foods. These are often high in sugar, unhealthy fats, and preservatives, all of which can disrupt hormone levels and contribute to weight gain. Opting for whole, natural foods is always a better choice for overall health and testosterone production.

By avoiding these testosterone-crushing foods, you can help support healthy testosterone levels and improve your overall health.

Check out this full list of foods to avoid . . .

## Dairy Products and Estrogen: How Prolactin Can Wreck Your Testosterone

Did you know that your favorite cheese or glass of milk might be the culprit behind your low testosterone levels?

Dairy products contain a hormone called prolactin, which can increase estrogen levels in your body and decrease testosterone production. Prolactin is typically associated with breastfeeding in women, but both men and women have this hormone in their bodies.

The problem with prolactin is that it stimulates estrogen production, which can negatively impact testosterone levels. One study found that men who consumed high amounts of dairy products had significantly higher levels of prolactin than men who did not consume dairy (15). The researchers linked this increase in prolactin to a decrease in testosterone levels.

In addition, dairy products are often high in saturated fats, which have also been shown to negatively impact testosterone levels. This is not to say that you need to cut dairy out of your diet entirely, but it is important to moderate your intake and choose low-fat options when possible.

By being aware of how dairy and prolactin can affect your testosterone levels, you can make more informed decisions about your diet and lifestyle choices to optimize your hormone production and overall health.

Dairy products account for 60 to 80 percent of the total estrogens that people consume, and many men simply don't realize how bad they really are, especially if you want to boost your testosterone levels.

## Polyunsaturated Vegetable Oils and Salad Dressings

Next on the list of foods to avoid are polyunsaturated vegetable oils and salad dressings. You don't want to include oils such as canola oil, flaxseed oil, safflower oil, sunflower oil, and soy oil in your diet plan. Many people worry about saturated fat intake, but the reality is that this type of fat is worse, especially for men.

For males, this type of fat can reduce testosterone levels, and because of the high amount of omega-6 fatty acids these oils possess, this can tilt your omega-3:omega-6 ratios in an unfavorable direction and lead to whole body inflammation.

Salad dressings are typically made from polyunsaturated vegetable oils and are also combined with other unwanted ingredients such as sugar and preservatives, so they should definitely not be on your list of foods to eat.

## Flaxseeds

Yes, flaxseeds – even though they are marketed as healthy. Although they can be healthy for women, for you, who are boosting your testosterone maximally, this is of concern. The issue with flaxseeds is, once again, the polyunsaturated fat content they possess, and the fact that they tend to have high estrogenic properties. They are a rich source of lignans, which are extremely estrogenic and may reduce total and free testosterone levels.

Men who consume large amounts of flaxseeds may start to see their estrogen levels increasing, and, therefore, notice their testosterone levels declining. In one study (11), when men consumed 30 grams of flaxseeds per day, they noted that their total testosterone levels dropped by approximately 15 percent while the total level of free testosterone declined by 20 percent.

Whether you are using whole flaxseeds, ground flaxseeds, or flaxseed oil, try to use these as little as possible.

## Mint

That peppermint gum you may be popping might freshen your breath, but it's not doing much for your testosterone levels. While the bit of mint in your gum may not have a negative effect, if you are in the habit of drinking spearmint or peppermint tea, you may want to curtail that habit.

In one study (12) subjects who consumed peppermint tea saw a 23 percent reduction in testosterone levels, while those who consumed spearmint tea noted a 51 percent decline. This would require you to consume about 5 grams of mint leaves steeped into a tea, to give you an idea of dosage.

Mint probably isn't something to stress out over too much – the mouthwash and toothpaste you use daily is fine (and should not be discontinued), but don't get into the habit of cooking with mint or drinking it regularly, or you may notice negative effects.

## Alcohol

If you enjoy having a drink, it's important to know that alcohol can be detrimental to your testosterone levels. Alcohol consumption can lower testosterone levels by increasing the conversion of testosterone to estrogen. This occurs because alcohol is converted into acetaldehyde in the liver, which is then converted into estradiol, a form of estrogen.

Additionally, alcohol has been shown to increase the production of the hormone prolactin, which also has an estrogenic effect, as mentioned earlier in this chapter. Prolactin is responsible for lactation in women, but it's present in both men and women. In men, it can lead to the suppression of testosterone production, which can negatively impact muscle mass, sex drive, and overall health. Research has also shown that alcohol can cause gynecomastia, a condition in which breast tissue grows in men (19), as well as testicular atrophy (13).

Several studies have suggested that chronic and excessive alcohol consumption can decrease testosterone levels in men. That's why I list alcohol as one of the testosterone-crushing worst offenders.

One study found that men with a history of chronic alcohol use had lower testosterone levels compared to nondrinkers and moderate drinkers (16). Another study found that acute alcohol consumption can decrease testosterone levels within hours after consumption and that the effects can last up to 24 hours (17).

Furthermore, alcohol consumption can increase the conversion of testosterone into estrogen by stimulating the activity of the aromatase enzyme, which converts testosterone into estrogen. This can lead to an increase in estrogen levels and a decrease in testosterone levels, which can negatively impact male health and fertility (18).

My advice is to avoid alcohol consumption until you hit your weight loss or testosterone goals and avoid these negative health consequences.

## Soy Products

Soy products are next on the no-no list of foods for men to eat if they hope to sustain higher testosterone levels. As noted earlier, soy products include soy milk, tofu, and edamame.

Soy is estrogenic in the body, so a heavy consumption of soy-rich foods can cause your estrogen levels to rise, which counteracts testosterone levels in the process.

Another manner in which soy will interact with testosterone production is that it is considered to be goitrogenic, which means that it disrupts the natural balance of the production of a critical thyroid regulating hormone. When your thyroid gland is not producing this hormone as it should this also leads to a further decrease in testosterone levels (14).

Unfortunately, soy protein ranks as one of the primary products that vegetarians consume as their protein source. If you are a vegetarian, you may want to refrain from consuming soy protein, and, instead, consider getting more of your protein from eggs and fish (if you are okay consuming those on your diet plan).

Quinoa and nuts will also provide small amounts of protein, so those are additional sources. Likewise, you may consider egg white or hemp protein powder as well. Just stay away from soy protein powder, as that will obviously not be any better than tofu or other soy-based foods.

## Trans Fats

We touched on trans fats briefly in an earlier chapter, but I need to mention it here again. If you want to optimize your testosterone levels, stay away from trans fats. Trans fats are a man-made type of fat that is found primarily in processed foods and are devastating for your health.

Often called *partially hydrogenated vegetable oil*, this type of fat has an extra hydrogen atom added to it. Food manufacturers like to use this type of fat, because it increases the shelf life of the products they are putting on the shelves, and because it often enhances the taste and texture of foods quite nicely.

But an intake of trans fats is linked to higher cholesterol levels, an increased risk of developing diabetes, reduced insulin sensitivity, higher total body inflammation levels, an increased risk of developing cancer, and lowered overall testosterone levels.

The most common foods that contain trans fats include doughnuts; baked goods such as cakes, pie crusts, biscuits, frozen pizza, cookies, and crackers; and margarine and spreads.

Just look for trans fats on the ingredient list, and, if you see it listed, stay away from that food. Even minor amounts (one gram or less) can be detrimental, so you really want to stay away from it entirely.

### Sugar

Sugar is currently being touted as one of the worst foods you can consume and for good reason – it is.

Most processed foods contain shocking amounts of sugar. When you consume processed foods, your body does not derive the nutrition that it would from wholesome food sources, and your blood glucose levels are going to rise and then fall dramatically.

This places your body under stress, and, as noted before, any stress on your body increases cortisol levels, which then hampers testosterone function.

Plus, sugar is a much greater threat to heart disease risk compared to the saturated fat that everyone avoids, so if you believe saturated fat is the enemy and are opting for processed, sugar-laden foods, you need to rethink this.

Those who consume high amounts of sugar are also at a great risk of weight gain. The more body fat you possess, the more estrogen you will secrete on a regular basis.

### Chemically Enhanced Meat

You should avoid chemically enhanced meat if you are hoping to boost your testosterone. This includes deli meat, sausages, bacon, and similar foods of this nature.

These foods contain toxic additives that may not only hamper testosterone production and mess with other hormones in the body, but they may be carcinogenic as well, especially if they are wrapped in plastic wrap, which is made from PVC and will leach into the food.

If you want deli meat, simply ask your butcher to shave your roasted chicken or beef fresh and then wrap it in brown paper or wax paper rather than in plastic. This works just as well for your lunches on the go.

### Chocolate

Chocolate is a much-loved food by many, but if you are hoping to boost your testosterone levels, it's yet another food that you'll want to think twice about.

While this food has been touted to be an aphrodisiac, it unfortunately also lowers testosterone levels in some men. This testosterone lowering is not straight across the board, however, so only some men appear to be impacted. It's worth avoiding if you can withstand the cravings.

### Microwave Popcorn

Finally, let's talk about the last item on our testosterone-crushing food list. Next time you're doing movie night, you may want to do without the microwave popcorn. While it is a lighter alternative to potato chips, it's really not an ideal option for anyone who is hoping to maintain favorable testosterone levels.

Microwave popcorn contains a chemical called perfluorooctanoic acid, which is found in the bag's lining, and it can be linked to a lowered sex drive as well as suppressed testosterone levels.

You don't have to give up popcorn on movie night! Just buy a container of popcorn kernels at the grocery store, then pop them on the stovetop the old-fashioned way. Add a bit of grass-fed butter and a dash of salt, and you have a healthy, high-fiber, movie-night snack.

So, there you have the main foods to avoid to keep your testosterone levels in check and reduce the chances that you start seeing negative implications in your day-to-day life with lowered testosterone levels.

### Conclusion

As you can see, your testosterone levels are very much under your control. Do not sit there and think that you have no influence over this. By making wise choices with your diet, you can most definitely help yourself see higher levels of testosterone and ensure you are moving forward with the progress you hope to obtain.

Just remember that almost everything you do on a daily basis is going to influence your testosterone levels, so don't think that just because you don't do one thing mentioned here, you might as well not bother with any of it. Even if you just make a few changes to your diet, that's better than doing nothing at all, and then, in time, you will see the positive benefits of those small changes.

## SECTION 3

# Implementing the Meta-Test Boost Nutrition System

**CHAPTER 9**
Welcome to the Meta-Test Boost Nutrition System 28-Day Meal Plan

**CHAPTER 10**
The 10 Commandments of the Meta-Test Boost Nutrition System

**CHAPTER 11**
Food List for a Healthy, Testosterone-Boosting Eating Plan

**CHAPTER 12**
Do-It-Yourself Meal Plan

**CHAPTER 13**
Done-For-You Meal Plan

CHAPTER 9

# Welcome to the Meta-Test Boost Nutrition System 28-Day Meal Plan

**YOU'VE MADE IT!** Take a deep breath, because now I am going to introduce you to the Meta-Test Boost Nutrition System 28-Day Meal Plan.

First, I want to let you know how proud I am of you now that you are here, because you are much more equipped with the information you need to "digest" the nutrition plan, so you can implement this starting today or tomorrow.

The focus of this meal plan is to help you turn up your fat loss into high gear and lose as much fat as you can in the next 28 days. More specifically, we are trying to cut your body fat percentage to 15 percent or as close to that as possible.

Please don't worry if you are far off from that right now. We will get you there in time.

This meal plan is going to give you the biggest bang for your buck, so to speak, in terms of the amount of effort you must put in, the focus you need to maintain, and the overall return of your investment.

Do it right, and I can assure you that you will be on track to seeing amazing results.

Essentially, we are focusing on establishing a simple weight-loss nutrition plan that you can stick with long term. As we all know, if you don't do it, it won't bring results. You need a diet that's workable in *your* life. And, by now, you know that I believe nutrition is the best way to boost your testosterone levels, so rest assured that the MTB Nutrition System takes this into account as well.

Remember, you cannot out-train a bad diet. No matter how many workouts you do, you will not get the results you want unless you are fueling your body with the right foods that help optimize your metabolism, incinerate body fat, build muscle, and elevate your natural testosterone levels.

### The Meta-Test Boost Nutrition System Will Help You . . .

1. Introduce foods into your diet that help boost your testosterone levels. Food can be that powerful. What you eat has a tremendous influence on your testosterone release.
2. Burn belly fat at a rapid pace. This is no "slow-and-steady" plan. You will start seeing results even from week one.
3. Learn which foods to eat to help decrease your estrogen levels as well as cortisol – two hormones that counteract testosterone and fat burning entirely.
4. Discover foods that will kick your metabolism into high gear.
5. Help stimulate the greatest possible growth of muscles while burning fat.

### NO Cheat Meals, NO Cheat Days, and NO Guilt-Free Meals

This book gives you everything you need to ensure your first 28 days on this plan are successful. Although you may opt to introduce a few guilt-free meals (cheat meals) in subsequent months – just a few! – the very first month using the Meta-Test Boost Nutrition System has no cheat meals, no cheat days, and no guilt-free meals.

Your goal for your initial month using the Meta-Test Boost Nutrition System is to focus on detoxing your body of the unhealthy foods and habits that you have adopted over the years. The goal is also to learn new, healthy eating behaviors and positive eating strategies.

This means there is no room for cheating, but, instead, focus on creating an environment that nourishes your body, your hormones, your energy, your mind, and your fat-loss journey. Plus, you will choose the foods from the Meta-Test Food List (Chapter 11) that you like and enjoy eating.

## The Meta-Test Boost Balanced Plate

Once again, we are not counting calories here but focusing on having a balanced plate with a nice mixture of proteins, starchy complex carbs, healthy fats, and vegetables/fruits with all of your main meals.

During this plan, you'll eat your three square meals a day – breakfast, lunch, and dinner – that is it. NO SNACKING!

If you feel like you need to snack in between meals, this means you are not eating enough complex carbs during your meals, so it's important that you have enough good carbs with each of your main meals.

Eating too often during the day will put stress on your body and digestive system. There are certain points in the day when it is more beneficial to eat more starchy complex carbs. In particular, it's helpful to eat after a workout when your body's glycogen stores are empty and need to be replenished with starchy carbs, so your body can continue its fat-burning metabolic process, continue its recovery from your workout, and ensure the protein you are eating gets to the muscles for growth.

## Meal Plan Breakdown

As you can see in the Meta-Test Boost Nutrition System diagram, each meal or smoothie will have a source of this macronutrient-balanced plate breakdown:

- Protein (20 percent)
- Starchy complex carbs (40 percent)
- Healthy fats (40 percent)
- Vegetables/fruits (unlimited, depends on the meal)

Follow this meal planning guide to ensure you have a balanced plate with the right amount of protein, starchy complex carbs, healthy fats, and veggies/fruits for every meal.

Below is an overview of the meal breakdown and why each fuel source is important.

### *Source of Protein*

You need a source of protein on your plate, preferably animal protein or whey protein, as they have the highest quality. Protein is the building block of our muscles, bones, and the metabolic processes that happen in the body. And since our body doesn't naturally produce protein, we need to get it from outside sources. Make sure there is a source of protein on your plate for every meal.

### *Source of Starchy Complex Carbs*

The next thing you need on your plate is a source of starchy complex carbs. This is super important, because good carbs are a source of energy that your body will use throughout the day. Eating starchy complex carbs helps with recovery after a workout, helps fuel muscle growth, and, most importantly, supports your thyroid, which is responsible for our fat-burning metabolism. When you don't have a starchy complex carb on your plate, you sabotage your diet and testosterone levels and force fat storage.

### *Source of Healthy Fats*

Next, you need a source of healthy fats. This should be a no-brainer for you, now that you know healthy fats have the source of good cholesterol that we need for testosterone production. Cholesterol is the precursor for testosterone production. Without it, no testosterone is released into your system.

### *Source of Vegetables/Fruits*

This is the last thing on your plate. Veggies and fruits have the micronutrients you need to balance your hormones and improve your health. Generally, you eat fruits in the morning with your breakfast or in your smoothies. But you can have them on your plate anytime. And veggies, especially greens, are essential throughout your day with all your meals.

## How to Choose Your Foods

To make nutrition simple and easy for you to follow, I use a process where you choose your Go-To Foods each week.

The first thing I want you to do is choose your Go-To Foods. These are the foods that you will eat the most during your meals. I've found that 90 percent of all people I work with do best when they can keep their meal plan simple and consistent. These foods will do just that.

So, think for a moment, which foods do you enjoy the most? Which do you tire of the least? Which are easy for you to purchase and prepare? You may want to review these food lists to select your Go-To Foods:

- Chapter 5's list of testosterone-boosting superfoods
- Chapter 8's list of foods that will crush your testosterone levels (you want to avoid these foods!)
- Chapter 11's extensive food list of proteins, healthy fats, starchy complex carbs, vegetables, fruits, and more for a healthy, testosterone-boosting eating plan

By now you probably have a few foods in mind. These are going to become your reliable foods. This isn't to say you can't add other healthy foods into the plan. Once you've mastered how this plan works and can do it without thought, then you can begin adding more variety, if you have the desire.

## Let's Show You What Your Day Should Look Like

I mentioned that you'll enjoy three square meals a day, but the Meta-Test Boost Nutrition System actually starts the minute you wake up. Let's step through your day . . .

### *Wake Up*

As soon as you wake up in the morning, the most crucial step is to hydrate your body with at least 16 to 32 ounces of water. Your body needs water, so it can process food. This also gives your metabolism a jump start and sets you up for great success as the day progresses.

### *Breakfast (Meal 1)*

Your breakfast meal will consist of a combination of starchy complex carbs along with a source of protein, healthy fats, and veggies/fruits, so you can begin the day in a fat-burning state. Of all the meals, people skip breakfast the most often. You don't want to do that. You should eat breakfast every day, and your breakfast should be automatic in terms of what you eat.

The less you must think, the more you can preserve your energy, concentration, and time. When you're trying to get out the door in a hurry, the last thing you want to think about is what's for breakfast.

If you don't want to cook breakfast, then my suggestion is to have a fat-burning smoothie. You'll find several delicious smoothie recipes in the Done-For-You Meal Plan in Chapter 13. And people get great results with the shakes in the morning, as they are fast and easy, and you can take them with you.

### *Lunch (Meal 2)*

Your lunch is going to be a more balanced meal with protein, starchy complex carbs, healthy fats, and vegetables/fruits. The purpose of your lunch is to help give you energy and sustain your metabolism throughout the day.

It's important that you prepare your lunch the night before your workday, so you don't leave home rushed and without it, or simply consider taking last night's dinner leftovers for lunch. This is one of the strategies I use to ensure that I don't have to think when it comes to lunch, and I don't get stuck eating something unhealthy.

### *Dinner (Meal 3)*

The goal of dinner is to have another healthy meal with protein, starchy complex carbohydrates, healthy fats, and vegetables/fruits. This is a great time to fire up the grill or make a delicious meal for your family. It's also a perfect time to make a little extra, so you have something prepared for lunch the next day.

## Important Meal Prep Notes

- Cook your food in bulk for the best results. (I cook on Sundays.) Meal prep is the key to success!
- Make sure to drink at least 16 ounces of water with each meal and in between meals.
- Do not eat anything after dinner and until breakfast. Remember, NO SNACKING!

## How to Determine Portion Sizes

Our food industry tends to double, triple, or even supersize servings, and restaurants are notorious for putting way more food on a plate than anyone should eat, leaving us perpetually overserved.

Unfortunately, many middle-aged men have visually adjusted to these big serving sizes and are unaware of what an accurate portion looks like.

If we can reprogram our brains to see healthy servings sizes, then maybe we won't be fooled when it comes to preparing our daily meal. We can set ourselves up for fat and weight loss while feeding our bodies nutrient-dense, testosterone-boosting foods.

Remember, with the Meta-Test Boost Nutrition System, you don't count calories but instead focus on creating balanced portions of macronutrients on your plate.

It can be hard to measure out every portion of food you eat. Yet there are some simple ways to know you are eating the right serving sizes. The MTB Nutrition System uses visual portion size indicators to help you when preparing your meals.

A *serving size* is a measured amount of food – 1 cup, 1 slice, 1 bag, and so forth – intended to be eaten at one time. It's the amount you'll see on a food label, and it's what the USDA uses in the Dietary Guidelines for Americans.

A *portion size*, by contrast, is the amount of food or drink you consume in one sitting, whether it's an entire rack of ribs or a smoothie. If you eat more or less than the recommended serving size, you may get either too much or too little of the nutrients and calories you need.

Use the portion size guide to help you match your portions to recommended serving sizes for the Meta-Test Boost Nutrition System.

How big is a portion? Use this easy guide to determine portion sizes for each meal's serving of starchy complex carbs, veggies/fruits, healthy fats, and protein.

## Key Guidelines: Daily Requirements for Macronutrients

So, how much are your daily requirements for protein, starchy complex carbs, healthy fats, and veggies/fruits? Each man has slightly different needs, because this depends on his total body weight as well as how active he is. Here are general guidelines to follow.

### *Proteins*

A male who seeks to increase testosterone levels while getting enough to grow muscle and burn fat should get 20 to 25 percent of his daily requirements through protein. This equates to 1.5 grams per kilogram of body weight or 0.7 grams per pound of body weight. Remember to get your protein through high-quality, grass-fed animal protein.

### *Healthy Fats*

These are important for the synthesis of testosterone and should be 25 to 40 percent of your daily requirements or 0.3 grams per pound of body weight. Be sure to focus on saturated and monounsaturated fats while adding polyunsaturated fats to the mix.

### *Starchy Complex Carbohydrates*

Carbs are crucial to producing testosterone and thyroid hormone output. Approximately 40 to 50 percent of your daily requirements should be from carbs, with 2.7 to 4.5 grams per pound of body weight. Ensure that you get your carbs through starchy complex carbs such as whole grains, not just vegetables and fruits.

### *Veggies/Fruits*

In addition to protein, healthy fats, and starchy complex carbohydrates, incorporating a generous amount of vegetables and fruits to round out your balanced plate meals is essential for optimal nutrition. Unlike the other macronutrients, there is no specific percentage or gram requirement for vegetables and fruits. Instead, you should see these nutrient-packed foods as unlimited additions to your plate.

Vegetables and fruits provide a wide array of vitamins, minerals, antioxidants, and dietary fiber, all of which are vital for men over 40. They support your immune function, promote healthy digestion, and reduce the risk of chronic diseases, such as heart disease, cancer, and cognitive decline.

To ensure a balanced plate, strive to fill at least half of your plate with a combination of vegetables and fruits during each meal. This way, you'll naturally increase your nutrient intake while keeping calories in check. Experiment with different cooking methods, such as roasting, steaming, or enjoying them raw in salads to maintain variety and enhance flavors.

Remember, you want to view vegetables and fruits as an essential and limitless resource on your journey toward optimal nutrition, increased testosterone, and overall well-being. Embrace their vibrant colors and flavors and make them a prominent part of your daily eating habits.

CHAPTER 10

# The 10 Commandments of the Meta-Test Boost Nutrition System

**WHEN IT COMES TO YOUR WEIGHT LOSS,** fat burning, muscle building, and balanced hormonal success, your nutrition lifestyle will make all the difference.

## You Can't Out-Train a Bad Diet!

No matter what – your sustained success will boil down to how committed and consistent you are with your nutrition plan.

You will need to master some nutrition fundamentals before you utilize more specific eating strategies like fasting to lose weight or eating to gain muscle. So, I have put together my Meta-Test Boost Nutrition System's 10 Commandments. These are the 10 guidelines that *everyone* (man or woman) must do to create a solid foundation for nutritional habits, regardless of your goals or what you are training for!

But keep in mind, these are *general* guidelines that are not specific to any medical condition, special population (like kids or elderly people), sport, or a goal related to physical activity (like bodybuilding).

These are simply foundational, good nutritional habits when following the Meta-Test Boost Nutrition System that you will need if you want to improve your health, performance, and physical appearance.

Ensure you follow these 10 Commandments.

### 1. Eat Three Meals Per Day

This is a principle that I will continue to hammer into you. The goal is to keep the body burning and your metabolism high. This means you need to eat three balanced plate meals per day. By doing this, you are ensuring your body gets the fuel it needs for energy, recovery, and fat loss. If you focus on breakfast, lunch, and dinner – or meal 1, meal 2, and meal 3 – that will help you stay focused on getting your three meals each day.

### 2. Each Meal Should Be a Balanced Plate

*This is non-negotiable.* This commandment is crucial to your weight loss, fat loss, testosterone production, health, energy, and hormone balance. Each meal or smoothie that you have throughout the day *must contain* a source of a starchy complex carbohydrate, healthy fat, high-quality protein, and either vegetables or fruits, depending on the meal. You don't have to count calories or weigh your food; you just simply must ensure you have a source of each of the macronutrients on every plate you eat or in every smoothie you make.

### 3. A Post-workout Meal is *Crucial* for Fat Loss

I will keep this short and to the point. Ensure you eat a balanced plate meal (with a little more carbs) within one and a half hours after your workout in order to replenish the glycogen stores that you drained during your workout and keep the metabolism going, so you can burn fat and not muscle. Do *not* just have a protein drink – that will not cut it! This is the most important meal of your workout day, and it's essential that you eat after your workout if you are serious about fat and weight loss.

### 4. Choose Your Go-To Foods for the Week

In order to keep things simple and allow you to follow a sustainable nutrition plan, one of the best strategies is to choose three to four Go-To Foods from each category of macronutrients (starchy complex carbs, healthy fats, protein, and veggies/fruits) that you want to eat throughout the week. You do not need to choose all your foods, but just the ones you will eat most frequently throughout that week. Plus, this will help make your food prep and grocery shopping easier each week.

## 5. Plan, Prepare, and Meal Prep

Remember that old saying: "Failing to plan is planning to fail!" Meal prep is another essential if you want to be successful with weight loss and nutrition. Creating a ritual of cooking up a batch of food on one day during the week (preferably a day off like Sunday) will dramatically increase the chances that you will stick with your nutrition plan.

Take an hour to prepare a big batch of protein sources, carbs, and even some veggies, or whatever recipes you want to prepare for the coming week; package them in individual storage containers; and put them in the fridge/freezer and eat them when you are ready. There is nothing like being prepared, especially when trying to follow new nutritional plans and guidelines.

## 6. Purge Your Cupboards

In Chapter 8, I gave you a list of foods and junk NOT to eat. Go through your pantry and get rid of all the BS. You need to throw away all the chips, crackers, cookies, ice cream, candy, soda, packaged meals, frozen dinners, and other processed crap. The best way to stay clear of foods and junk that you should not eat is to get these foods out of the house. Make sure you purge your cupboards. Get rid of all those unhealthy foods and overstock with healthy choices. If it's not in the house, you won't eat it. Conversely, if good stuff is handy, you will eat it – and probably enjoy it!

## 7. Drink One Gallon of Water per Day

I ask everyone this question: "Do you drink a lot of water?" Everyone says the same thing: "I drink tons of water; that's all I drink." Then, when I tell them they should be drinking at least one gallon per day, they step back and say, "That much?" My answer is "Yes, that is what is called a lot of water."

If you are not drinking at least one gallon of water per day, then you are not getting enough water, especially if you are working out. Drinking a lot of water helps to accelerate fat loss and dehydration. So, start drinking water!

### 8. Drinking a Post-workout Protein Shake is Key

If you want to start the recovery process, feed your muscles, and burn fat, then having a post-workout protein shake is super important. Do not get this mixed up with your post-workout meal – this is just a simple shake containing New Zealand whey protein powder and BCAAs powder mixed with water. That's it. This will start the recovery process while you stretch, shower, and prepare your post-workout meal. This protein shake is a gamechanger!

### 9. Absolutely NO Alcohol or Cheat Meals During Your First Month on Your Nutrition System

The goal in the first month of this nutrition system and lifestyle is completely detoxing your body of the unhealthy foods that do the most damage to your body, system, weight loss goals, hormones, and overall health. That means NO cheat meals for at least 28 days.

Drinking alcohol is one of the biggest reasons people cannot lose weight! Eliminating it completely will give your body the detoxification it needs while you will lose a *ton* of weight and feel great!

### 10. Supplement Wisely

Supplements are amazing, as they plug in any deficiencies you may have with your nutrition and will also help with your recovery process after workouts. But they are *not* a replacement for your nutrition. Just add a supplement to your nutrition plan to ensure you accelerate your health and results. Add supplements slowly, so you are not wasting your hard-earned cash. Start with a high-quality grass-fed whey protein powder, multivitamins, BCAAs, and omega-3s.

### Bonus: Eat a Lot of Vegetables and Fruits

Duh.

Low in calories and dense in nutrition (vitamins, minerals, and antioxidants), vegetables and fruits are vital for increasing energy, reducing the risk of various diseases, and increasing your metabolism.

Green vegetables are generally filled with calcium, magnesium, iron, potassium, zinc, and vitamins A, C, E, and K. And they help strengthen the blood and respiratory systems. Sweet vegetables are great, because they help curb your appetite and help reduce the cravings for sweets like cookies and chocolate.

Make sure to have a wide variety of fruits! Fruits are great breakfast foods, because many contain fiber (which helps you poop and clear your system), vitamins, and antioxidants.

Plus, a good number of vegetables and fruits can help in your recovery as well due to the high volume of nutrients.

Well, there you have it.

Simple.

Follow these 10 Commandments to the "T" especially in your first couple of months on this nutrition plan. This will completely change your life while making prep and eating super easy, simple, and successful!

## GET IT DONE!

## CHAPTER 11

# Food List for a Healthy, Testosterone-Boosting Eating Plan

**IT'S TIME TO TAKE CONTROL OF YOUR KITCHEN** and your health to finally melt away stubborn belly fat, build muscle, fight the aging process, increase energy, and boost your testosterone. Remember, the Meta-Test Boost Nutrition System is your key to naturally boosting your *metabolism* and *testosterone.*

In this chapter, you'll learn details about a healthy, testosterone-boosting, fat-burning eating plan that is not boring or repetitive. As you will see in the master list below, eating testosterone-boosting foods does not mean eating the same skinless chicken breast night after night, wishing you can have something more delicious and satisfying.

Eating for your health is actually eating satisfying and delicious foods, which you will see in the list. The best diet consists of fresh, unprocessed foods with ingredients you can recognize, raised or grown as naturally as possible.

What you will *not* see on this list are the foods that combat our number-one, manly hormone testosterone and that lower or stop its production.

The goal is to lower your estrogen and cortisol levels and balance insulin, while decreasing inflammation, supporting your thyroid (fat-burning metabolism), and boosting your T-levels.

It's time to eliminate those fake, processed "diet" convenience foods: frozen, packaged, processed "weight loss" dinners; artificial sweeteners; sugar-laden yogurt; processed "energy bars"; soy products; fake meat products (usually made with processed soy); diet shakes; and more.

This artificial food is fooling you and your body, and it's adversely affecting your hormones and internal biochemistry. This food usually ends up making you addicted to it. You gain weight and feel terrible, so don't be fooled!

The Meta-Test Boost Nutrition System focuses on fueling your body with real, whole foods that are *really* good for your body and your mind.

Real, whole foods usually contain one ingredient and are packed with thousands of vital nutrients the body needs and craves.

- Eggs are one ingredient.
- An apple is one ingredient.
- Nuts have one ingredient.
- Grass-fed meat has one ingredient.
- Vegetables, fruits, and seeds have one ingredient.

And then you also have healthy foods such as guacamole, which are combinations of one-ingredient foods.

When you feed your body what it really craves – real nutrition – your cravings for junk food go away. So does your constant hunger.

*The Meta-Test Boost Nutrition System is not about dieting but about leading a sustainable, healthy, lean-eating lifestyle while feasting on delicious foods day in and day out!*

Below is the master list of testosterone-boosting foods you can include in your nutrition and diet plans from this day forward. Stick to this list, and this list only, if you want to focus on boosting your testosterone. These foods are backed by research, science, and studies to help promote and increase testosterone while lowering testosterone killing hormones like estrogen, cortisol, and insulin, along with keeping inflammation down.

Stock your fridge, freezer, and cupboards with these testosterone-boosting foods!

## Choose Your Go-To Foods from These Lists

What I want you to do is choose your Go-To Foods for the four categories of macronutrients that you'll use for the next four weeks: protein, starchy complex carbs, healthy fats, and veggies/fruits. Remember, the goal is to create a balanced plate with all four macronutrients for every meal. I've also included recommendations for drinks and teas, herbs and spices, condiments, and a few other miscellaneous foods.

These foods should be, as I mentioned above, foods you enjoy eating, foods you know how to cook, and foods you don't tire of easily. You'll be eating them often, so you don't want to find that you're getting sick of them two weeks into the plan.

What I want you to do right now is choose four foods from each category listed below.

### *Proteins*

Eat lean, protein-rich foods (typically meat, poultry, and fish) in every meal. Focus on grass-fed meats, but don't obsess. Eat pork, turkey, and chicken in moderation (they contain more omega-6 fats). Opt for wild-caught fish and free-run, organic eggs.

- Chicken
- Beef
- Whole eggs (organic)
- Egg whites
- Turkey breast
- Turkey bacon
- Bacon
- Bison
- Grass-fed beef jerky
- Minced meat
- Venison
- Elk
- Duck

- Lamb
- Pork
- Organ meat
- Wild-caught salmon
- Wild-caught tuna
- Oysters
- Lobster
- Crab
- Halibut
- Shrimp
- Mackerel
- Sardines
- Tilapia
- Plain Greek yogurt
- Beef broth
- Lamb (plus one serving fat)
- Pork
- Organ meat
- Grass-fed whey protein powder

### *Starchy Complex Carbs*

Note that for all the carbohydrate options listed below, one serving will count as 1/2 cup of cooked food or approximately one cupped hand's worth, unless otherwise indicated.

These will be our main carbohydrate sources on this program. Foods like sweet potatoes, jasmine rice, quinoa, and oatmeal are all fantastic choices.

- White rice
- Jasmine rice
- Basmati rice
- Black rice
- Steal-cut oats

- Legumes
- Black beans
- Sweet potato
- White potato
- Red potato
- Squash
- Kidney beans
- Lima beans
- Ezekiel bread
- Gluten-free whole tortilla

### *Healthy Fats*

Note that one serving will count as one tablespoon of fat for butters or oils and one ounce for nuts and cheese. These foods are made up of almost exclusively healthy fat.

Keep in mind, some fattier cuts of meat have *both* protein and fat. Since we use leaner meats in the MTB Nutrition System, we need to add healthy fats in the form of good oils (extra virgin olive oil, virgin coconut oil, macadamia nut oil), whole eggs, and any kind of nuts or seeds.

- Raw nut butter
- Walnuts
- Cashews
- Avocado
- Brazil nuts
- Ricotta cheese
- Macadamia nuts
- Almonds
- Pistachios
- Avocado oil
- Sunflower seeds
- Pumpkin seeds

- Extra virgin olive oil
- Coconut oil
- Grass-fed butter
- MCT oil
- MCT oil powder
- Argan oil
- Feta cheese
- Pine nuts
- Ghee

### *Vegetables*

These vegetables are loaded with fiber and *do not* have a lot of carbohydrates. Fibrous vegetables include almost everything green, especially broccoli, Brussels sprouts, asparagus, and mixed salad.

- Broccoli
- Asparagus
- Kale
- White button mushrooms
- Spinach
- Leafy greens
- Cauliflower
- Maca root
- Brussels sprouts
- Cabbage
- Zucchini
- Okra
- Peas
- Bell pepper
- Celery
- Radish

- Artichoke
- Scallions
- Cucumber
- Onion
- Tomato

### *Fruits*

Choose from these fruits for your eating plan. Remember not to load up on fruit but eat small amounts as supportive foods.

- Apple
- Banana
- Orange
- Grapefruit
- Other citrus fruits
- Mango
- Pomegranate
- Cranberries
- Grapes
- Plum
- Pineapple
- Blueberries
- Cherries
- Avocado
- Goji berries
- Watermelon
- Figs
- Cantaloupe
- Mangosteen

### *Drinks and Teas*

Here are the drinks on the Meta-Test Boost Nutrition System:

- Water
- Black coffee
- Organic green tea
- Herbal teas
- Almond milk
- Pomegranate juice
- Coconut juice – unsweetened

### *Herbs and Spices*

Every time you flavor your meals with herbs or spices you are super-boosting your food without adding a single calorie. Herbs and spices add tons of extra flavor, and when combined with other foods, they actually boost the natural antioxidant and anti-inflammatory power of the food.

Herbs and spices are also thermogenic, which means they naturally help increase metabolism to allow you to burn fat.

Some spices are also good at regulating blood sugar and controlling insulin. When your blood sugar is well controlled, you are more likely to burn fat than store calories as excess weight.

- Real salt
- Freshly ground pepper
- Hot pepper flakes
- Ginger
- Rosemary
- Basil
- Cumin
- Turmeric
- Sage
- Lemongrass

- Nutmeg
- Cayenne
- Coriander
- Cinnamon
- Oregano
- Garlic
- Thyme
- Marjoram
- Chili powder
- Curry powder
- Mucuna pruriens

### *Condiments*

- Mustard
- Hummus
- Salsa
- Hot sauce
- Tabasco sauce
- Organic almond butter
- Nut butters
- Raw honey
- Stevia sweetener
- Vinaigrette salad dressing
- Nutritional yeast

### *Other*

- Raw cacao
- Wheat bran
- Baking soda
- Dark chocolate in moderation
- Almond meal

## CHAPTER 12

# Do-It-Yourself Meal Plan

**WELCOME TO THE HEART** of the Meta-Test Boost Nutrition System – the meal plans! In this section, I will provide you with everything you need to make meal planning easy and effective.

Whether you're a DIY type who wants to customize your plans using the food list or you prefer a done-for-you approach where I tell you exactly what to eat and when, I have got you covered.

Get ready to transform your body, boost your testosterone, and optimize your health with the power of the Meta-Test Boost Nutrition System.

I understand that you may have your own food preferences, so a plan that allows you to personalize your menu while still ensuring you get the correct fat-burning nutrients in each meal is your ticket to success.

While some people love having everything laid out for them, this is not what everyone prefers. If you like creating your own meals and picking your foods every time you eat, then you need something else.

With this 28-day, customizable, Do-It-Yourself Meal Plan, you will have the guidance to know what to eat and when, but then the rest will be up to you.

Sound too complicated? It's not. All you need to do is follow my simple formula and everything is laid out for you. This makes fat loss a breeze and still gives you the flexibility to enjoy the testosterone-boosting foods you want to eat.

On this plan, you'll be eating three meals each day – breakfast, lunch, and dinner.

Your body is primed to burn fat at certain points of the day as long as you give it the right nutrients. So, this is what my MTB Nutrition System focuses on – giving you what you need when you need it. If you manage to do this, fat loss becomes much easier.

In the morning, you'll eat fewer carbohydrates, and then, as the day gets moving along, your meals will be more balanced, including proteins, carbohydrates, and dietary fats.

I highly suggest that, as much as possible, you try to follow a ritual for your meal plan. You want to aim to eat your meals at about the same time each day, so you can stick to this system.

## How to Use the DIY Meal Plan

The Do-It-Yourself (DIY) Meal Plan lets you pick and choose the right foods and put them into your own personalized meal plan and menu. You can now create an effective, fat-burning, and testosterone-boosting nutrition plan that allows you to see the best possible results as long as you follow our easy-to-use guidelines.

## Here's What You Should Be Doing

1. Review the meal planning guide, portion size graphic, and guidelines for daily requirements in Chapter 9 to identify your requirements for each meal.
2. Review the food lists in Chapter 11 and select which foods you want to eat and determine the right quantity to meet your goals.
3. Even though you're a DIY guy, you may want to review the Done-For-You Meal Plan in the next chapter for great ideas to ensure you create a nutritious, delicious, balanced plate for every breakfast, lunch, and dinner.

| BREAKFAST | |
|---|---|
| **Protein (P)** | 2 servings |
| **Starchy Carbs (C)** | 1 serving |
| **Healthy Fats (F)** | 2 servings |
| **Veggies/Fruits (V)** | 2 servings |

| LUNCH | |
|---|---|
| **Protein (P)** | 1-2 servings |
| **Starchy Carbs (C)** | 1-2 servings |
| **Healthy Fats (F)** | 2 servings |
| **Veggies/Fruits (V)** | 2 servings |

| DINNER | |
|---|---|
| **Protein (P)** | 1-2 servings |
| **Starchy Carbs (C)** | 1-2 servings |
| **Healthy Fats (F)** | 2 servings |
| **Veggies/Fruits (V)** | 2 servings |

## My Stick-With-It Suggestion

Aim to make Sunday (or another day) your meal prep day, so you are ready to go throughout the week, and your meals won't require extra preparation when you are rushed.

Easy enough, right?

## Meal Plan Template

Using the following template, you can begin to build your 28-day meal plan. Note that we have not included how many numbers of each macro to have (with the exception of your breakfast meal, as you are making it lower carb, so it's only one carb serving at this time). This is because it's up to you to figure out how many servings you should eat each day based on the guidelines for daily requirements of macronutrients discussed in Chapter 9.

- Wake up – Drink 32 ounces of water
- Breakfast – P/1C/F/V
- Lunch – P/C/F/V
- Dinner – P/C/F/V

Notice how each meal should have a balanced mix of macronutrients – a balanced plate – which will help sustain you until your next meal.

That's it!

Once you calculate how many servings you should have at each meal, you're ready to start having fun and choosing your foods.

Here are some additional tips that can help you take this one step further:

- Aim to drink at least 16 ounces of water in between your meals. This will help ensure you are staying well hydrated and will prevent hunger as well.
- Avoid eating anything after dinner and before breakfast. This time is fasting time.
- Don't overcomplicate things! It's often best to just choose a few foods from each category to work with.
- Cook your food in bulk whenever possible.
- Don't beat yourself up if you slip up. Remember, it's how you get back on track that will really matter at the end of the day.

## Food Journal Template to Plan Each Day's Menu

Below is a template food journal you can print and use to help you plan your menu for each day. To help you get started, you can review the Done-For-You Meal Plan menus in the next chapter – you can use and adjust each of the 28 days' menus as you like. As you complete each day's food journal, be sure to write down the number of servings you plan to have at each meal and the food you will prep and eat to make up that serving. Remember, planning and preparation will be your keys to success!

| Meal | ____P Servings | ____C Serving | ____F Serving | ____V Serving |
|---|---|---|---|---|
| Breakfast | | | | |
| **Meal** | **____P Servings** | **____C Serving** | **____F Serving** | **____V Serving** |
| Lunch | | | | |
| **Meal** | **____P Servings** | **____C Serving** | **____F Serving** | **____V Serving** |
| Dinner | | | | |

## CHAPTER 13

# Done-For-You Meal Plan

**IF YOU LIKE TAKING THE GUESSWORK OUT** of what to eat and when, you'll love this 28-day Meta-Test Boost Nutrition System Done-for-You Meal Plan. It lays out 28 days of delicious, testosterone-boosting meals, all ready to go, no thinking required.

Each day in this meal plan contains three meals, so you never have to worry about being hungry. You'll get breakfast, lunch, and dinner, all of which go hand in hand with our protocol and recommendations.

Note that, because we can't make a meal plan for absolutely everyone, you will have to customize the portion size, so it meets your own specific needs. This will make it absolutely perfect for you. Of course, if you have any food allergies or sensitivities, you will want to take this into consideration as well.

Keep in mind that this plan is flexible, so feel free to rearrange or swap out meals according to your own preferences. Love one breakfast more than others? No problem! Just eat that breakfast a few more times during the week. The beauty of a good diet plan is that you can make it work for you.

This means you aren't confined to only eating the exact foods that are given to you, but, rather, you are able to pick and choose the foods you enjoy and eat those more often. We all know that enjoying our diet is key to sticking with it, and sticking with it is key to success.

I hope you enjoy these meal plans and experience the great health benefits, increased vitality, and strength that comes along with eating healthy, natural, testosterone-boosting foods.

You should start to see a difference after only a few short days, so don't delay getting started. You can start today or tomorrow!

## About This Plan

On this plan, you'll be eating three meals each day – breakfast, lunch, and dinner. Remember, there are no snacks or cheat meals. Your three square meals will provide plenty of calories, so you won't feel hungry throughout the day.

Your morning meal will be lower in carbohydrates than your afternoon and dinner meals, and this is to help you burn fat more effectively in the morning. Your body runs better when you have fewer lower-carb foods at this time of the day.

I highly recommend that you establish a good ritual when it comes to your meal plan, so you are eating at similar times during the day, and it becomes almost automatic – something you can do without thought. The less thinking you have to do on this diet plan, the easier it will be. That's the whole point of this Done-For-You approach. Everything is laid out for you, so all you need to do is "plug and play," more or less.

A typical day would look like this:

| | |
|---|---|
| **6:45 a.m.** | Wake up and drink 16 to 32 ounces of water |
| **7:00 a.m.** | Have your breakfast or a breakfast smoothie |
| **12:00 p.m.** | Eat lunch |
| **7:00 p.m.** | Have your dinner |

Remember, the quality of food you put into your body will have a direct influence on what you get out of your body. If you put junk in, you're going to feel miserable, have low energy, and won't see the results you hope to see. If you put in high-quality food, on the other hand, you're going to see better fat loss and feel better as well.

Keep in mind that you may require more or fewer calories (and the corresponding macronutrients) while on this plan, so you will need to adjust and adapt this plan for your needs accordingly.

## Done-For-You Meal Plan

In the following pages, you'll find your Done-For-You Meal Plan for breakfast, lunch, and dinner for four weeks. Follow it as is, or swap certain foods for similar foods, if desired. Do try to keep the order of meals the same, however. In other words, don't swap a lunch menu for a dinner menu. And make sure you have a source of protein, starchy complex carb, healthy fat, and veggies/fruits – a balanced plate – at each meal.

## WEEK 1

| MONDAY | |
|---|---|
| **BREAKFAST** | Breakfast Shake: 1-2 scoops whey protein powder, 1 cup raw steel cut oats, 1 cup spinach, 1 frozen banana, 2 tbsp. almond butter; mix with water and ice cubes |
| **LUNCH** | 6 oz. grilled chicken breast, 1 1/2 cups jasmine rice, 1 cup steamed asparagus, 2 tbsp. olive oil, 1/2 avocado |
| **DINNER** | 6 oz. grilled salmon, 1 to 1 1/2 cups jasmine rice, 1 cup stir-fried vegetables, 1/2 avocado |

| TUESDAY | |
|---|---|
| **BREAKFAST** | Breakfast Shake: 1-2 scoops whey protein powder, 1 cup kale leaves, 1 cup raw steel cut oats, 1 cup frozen blueberries, 3 tbsp. unsweetened coconut flakes, 1 tsp. almond butter; mix with water and ice cubes |
| **LUNCH** | 6 oz. wild-caught fish, 1 1/2 cups baked sweet potatoes, 2 cups spinach salad, 2 tbsp. olive oil-based dressing, and 1/2 avocado |
| **DINNER** | 6 oz. grilled pork tenderloin, 1 cup mashed sweet potatoes, 1 cup steamed cauliflower with olive oil, and 1/2 avocado |

| WEDNESDAY | |
|---|---|
| **BREAKFAST** | Alpha Oats Breakfast – 1 cup cooked steel cut oats, 1 scoop whey protein, 1/2 cup blueberries, 1 sliced banana, 1 tbsp. almond butter |
| **LUNCH** | 6 oz. grilled chicken, 1 1/2 cups jasmine rice, 2 cups steamed broccoli with 1/2 avocado |

| | |
|---|---|
| **DINNER** | 6 oz. grass-fed steak, 1 cup mashed sweet potatoes with grass-fed butter, spinach salad with 1/2 avocado |

| **THURSDAY** | |
|---|---|
| **BREAKFAST** | Chocolate Cashew Oats Breakfast Bowl – 1 cup cooked steel cut oats, 1 scoop chocolate whey protein, 1/2 cup blackberries, 1/2 cup raspberries, 1 sliced banana, handful cashews |
| **LUNCH** | 6 oz. salmon grilled and served with 1 1/2 cups mashed sweet potatoes and 1 cup sautéed green beans with 1/2 avocado |
| **DINNER** | 1 can crab meat, 1/4 cup cooked steel cut oats, 1 whole egg, 1/2 diced onion, pan fried into a burger; serve with 1/2 cup jasmine rice, mustard, and steamed broccoli with 1/2 avocado |

| **FRIDAY** | |
|---|---|
| **BREAKFAST** | Breakfast Shake: 1-2 scoops whey protein powder, 1 cup kale leaves, 1 cup raw steel cut oats, 1 tsp. almond butter, 1 cup frozen blueberries, 3 tbsp. unsweetened coconut flakes; mix with water and ice cubes |
| **LUNCH** | 6 oz. grilled chicken breast, 1 1/2 cups jasmine rice, 1 cup steamed asparagus, 2 tbsp. olive oil, 1/2 avocado |
| **DINNER** | 6 oz. grilled pork tenderloin, 1 cup mashed sweet potatoes, 1 cup steamed cauliflower with olive oil and 1/2 avocado |

| SATURDAY | |
|---|---|
| **BREAKFAST** | 1 cup egg whites with 2-4 whole eggs scrambled with 1 cup diced vegetables, handful spinach and tomatoes fried in coconut oil; serve with 2 slices of Ezekiel bread, 1 avocado, and 1/2 cup berries on the side |
| **LUNCH** | 6 oz. grilled shrimp, 1 pita, 1 cup mixed greens, 1/2 sliced avocado, mustard, 1 cup blueberries |
| **DINNER** | 1 cup egg whites with 2 whole eggs scrambled with 1 cup diced vegetables in 1 tbsp. olive oil; serve with 1 cup pan-fried pre-baked sweet potatoes |

| SUNDAY | |
|---|---|
| **BREAKFAST** | 4 whole egg omelet, with spinach/kale, tomatoes; serve with 3 pieces of turkey bacon, 2 slices of Ezekiel bread with grass-fed butter, and 1/2 avocado |
| **LUNCH** | 6 oz. grilled chicken with 2 slices Ezekiel bread, mustard, tomato, lettuce, and cucumber topped with 1/2 avocado; serve with 1 cup strawberries |
| **DINNER** | 6 oz. baked salmon with 1 cup baked sweet potatoes and 1 cup green beans; serve with 1/2 avocado |

## WEEK 2

| MONDAY | |
|---|---|
| **BREAKFAST** | Breakfast Shake: 1-2 scoops whey protein powder, 1 cup raw steel cut oats, 1 cup spinach, 1 frozen banana, 2 tbsp. almond butter; mix with water and ice cubes |

| | |
|---|---|
| **LUNCH** | 6 oz. grilled chicken breast, 1 1/2 cups jasmine rice, 1 cup steamed asparagus, 2 tbsp. olive oil, 1/2 avocado |
| **DINNER** | 6 oz. grilled salmon, 1 to 1 1/2 cups jasmine rice, 1 cup stir-fried vegetables, 1/2 avocado |

| TUESDAY | |
|---|---|
| **BREAKFAST** | Breakfast Shake: 1-2 scoops whey protein powder, 1 cup kale leaves, 1 cup raw steel cut oats, 1 cup frozen blueberries, 3 tbsp. unsweetened coconut flakes, 1 tsp. almond butter; mix with water and ice cubes |
| **LUNCH** | 6 oz. wild-caught fish, 1 1/2 cups baked sweet potatoes, 2 cups spinach salad, 2 tbsp. olive oil-based dressing, and 1/2 avocado |
| **DINNER** | 6 oz. grilled pork tenderloin, 1 cup mashed sweet potatoes, 1 cup steamed cauliflower with olive oil, and 1/2 avocado |

| WEDNESDAY | |
|---|---|
| **BREAKFAST** | Alpha Oats Breakfast – 1 cup cooked steel cut oats, 1 scoop whey protein, 1/2 cup blueberries, 1 sliced banana, 1 tbsp. almond butter |
| **LUNCH** | 6 oz. grilled chicken, 1 1/2 cups jasmine rice, 2 cups steamed broccoli with 1/2 avocado |
| **DINNER** | 6 oz. grass-fed steak, 1 cup mashed sweet potatoes with grass-fed butter, spinach salad with 1/2 avocado |

| THURSDAY | |
|---|---|
| **BREAKFAST** | Chocolate Cashew Oats Breakfast Bowl – 1 cup cooked steel cut oats,1 scoop chocolate whey protein, 1/2 cup blackberries, 1/2 cup raspberries, 1 sliced banana, handful cashews |
| **LUNCH** | 6 oz. salmon grilled and served with 1 1/2 cups mashed sweet potatoes and 1 cup sautéed green beans with 1/2 avocado |
| **DINNER** | 1 can crab meat, 1/4 cup cooked steel cut oats, 1 whole egg, 1/2 diced onion, pan fried into a burger; serve with 1/2 cup jasmine rice, mustard, and steamed broccoli with 1/2 avocado |

| FRIDAY | |
|---|---|
| **BREAKFAST** | Breakfast Shake: 1-2 scoops whey protein powder, 1 cup kale leaves, 1 cup raw steel cut oats, 1 tsp. almond butter, 1 cup frozen blueberries, 3 tbsp. unsweetened coconut flakes; mix with water and ice cubes |
| **LUNCH** | 6 oz. grilled chicken breast, 1 1/2 cups jasmine rice, 1 cup steamed asparagus, 2 tbsp. olive oil, 1/2 avocado |
| **DINNER** | 6 oz. grilled pork tenderloin, 1 cup mashed sweet potatoes, 1 cup steamed cauliflower with olive oil, 1/2 avocado |

| SATURDAY | |
|---|---|
| **BREAKFAST** | 1 cup egg whites with 2-4 whole eggs scrambled with 1 cup diced vegetables, handful spinach and tomatoes fried in coconut oil; serve with 2 slices of Ezekiel bread, 1 avocado, and 1/2 cup berries on the side |
| **LUNCH** | 6 oz. grilled shrimp, 1 pita, 1 cup mixed greens, 1/2 sliced avocado, mustard, 1 cup blueberries |

| | |
|---|---|
| **DINNER** | 1 cup egg whites with 2 whole eggs scrambled with 1 cup diced vegetables in 1 tbsp. olive oil; serve with 1 cup pan-fried pre-baked sweet potatoes |

| SUNDAY | |
|---|---|
| **BREAKFAST** | 4 whole egg omelet, with spinach/kale, tomatoes; serve with 3 pieces of turkey bacon with 2 slices of Ezekiel bread with grass-fed butter, and 1/2 avocado |
| **LUNCH** | 6 oz. grilled chicken served with 2 slices Ezekiel bread, mustard, tomato, lettuce, and cucumber topped with 1/2 avocado; serve with 1 cup strawberries |
| **DINNER** | 6 oz. baked salmon with 1 cup mashed sweet potatoes and 1 cup green beans; serve with 1/2 avocado |

## WEEK 3

| MONDAY | |
|---|---|
| **BREAKFAST** | Breakfast Shake: 1-2 scoops whey protein powder, 1 cup raw steel cut oats, 1 cup spinach, 1 frozen banana, 2 tbsp. almond butter; mix with water and ice cubes |
| **LUNCH** | 6 oz. grilled chicken breast, 1 1/2 cups jasmine rice, 1 cup steamed asparagus, 2 tbsp. olive oil, 1/2 avocado |
| **DINNER** | 6 oz. grilled salmon, 1 to 1 1/2 cups jasmine rice, 1 cup stir-fried vegetables, 1/2 avocado |

| TUESDAY | |
|---|---|
| **BREAKFAST** | Breakfast Shake: 1-2 scoops whey protein powder, 1 cup kale leaves,1 cup raw steel cut oats, 1 cup frozen blueberries, 3 tbsp. unsweetened coconut flakes, 1 tsp. almond butter; mix with water and ice cubes |
| **LUNCH** | 6 oz. wild-caught fish, 1 1/2 cups baked sweet potatoes, 2 cups spinach salad, 2 tbsp. olive oil-based dressing, and 1/2 avocado |
| **DINNER** | 6 oz. grilled pork tenderloin, 1 cup mashed sweet potatoes, 1 cup steamed cauliflower with olive oil, and 1/2 avocado |

| WEDNESDAY | |
|---|---|
| **BREAKFAST** | Alpha Oats Breakfast – 1 cup cooked steel cut oats, 1 scoop whey protein, 1/2 cup blueberries, 1 sliced banana, 1 tbsp. almond butter |
| **LUNCH** | 6 oz. grilled chicken, 1 1/2 cups jasmine rice, 2 cups steamed broccoli with 1/2 avocado |
| **DINNER** | 6 oz. grass-fed steak, 1 cup mashed sweet potatoes with grass-fed butter, spinach salad with 1/2 avocado |

| THURSDAY | |
|---|---|
| **BREAKFAST** | Chocolate Cashew Oats Breakfast Bowl – 1 cup cooked steel cut oats, 1 scoop chocolate whey protein, 1/2 cup blackberries, 1⁄2 cup raspberries, 1 sliced banana, handful cashews |
| **LUNCH** | 6 oz. salmon grilled and served with 1 1/2 cups mashed sweet potatoes and 1 cup sautéed green beans with 1/2 avocado |

| | |
|---|---|
| **DINNER** | 1 can crab meat, 1/4 cup cooked steel cut oats, 1 whole egg, 1/4 diced onion, pan fried into a burger. Served with 1/2 cup jasmine rice, mustard, and steamed broccoli with 1/2 avocado |

| **FRIDAY** | |
|---|---|
| **BREAKFAST** | Breakfast Shake: 1-2 scoops whey protein powder, 1 cup kale leaves,1 cup raw steel cut oats, 1 tsp. almond butter, 1 cup frozen blueberries, 3 tbsp. unsweetened coconut flakes; mix with water and ice cubes |
| **LUNCH** | 6 oz. grilled chicken breast, 1 1/2 cups jasmine rice, 1 cup steamed asparagus, 2 tbsp. olive oil, 1/2 avocado |
| **DINNER** | 6 oz. grilled pork tenderloin, 1 cup mashed sweet potatoes, 1 cup steamed cauliflower with olive oil, and 1/2 avocado |

| **SATURDAY** | |
|---|---|
| **BREAKFAST** | 1 cup egg whites with 2-4 whole eggs scrambled with 1 cup diced vegetables, handful spinach and tomatoes fried in coconut oil; serve with 2 slices of Ezekiel bread, 1 avocado, and 1/2 cup berries on the side |
| **LUNCH** | 6 oz. grilled shrimp, 1 pita, 1 cup mixed greens, 1/2 sliced avocado, mustard, 1 cup blueberries |
| **DINNER** | 1 cup egg whites with 2 whole eggs scrambled with 1 cup diced vegetables in 1 tbsp. olive oil; serve with 1 cup pan-fried pre-baked sweet potatoes |

| SUNDAY | |
|---|---|
| **BREAKFAST** | 4 whole egg omelet, with spinach/kale, tomatoes served with 3 pieces of turkey bacon with 2 slices of Ezekiel bread with grass-fed butter, and 1/2 avocado |
| **LUNCH** | 6 oz. grilled chicken served with 2 slices Ezekiel bread, mustard, tomato, lettuce, and cucumber topped with 1/2 avocado; serve with 1 cup strawberries |
| **DINNER** | 6 oz. baked salmon with 1 cup mashed sweet potatoes and 1 cup green beans; serve with 1/2 avocado |

## WEEK 4

| MONDAY | |
|---|---|
| **BREAKFAST** | Breakfast Shake: 1-2 scoops whey protein powder, 1 cup raw steel cut oats, 1 cup spinach, 1 frozen banana, 2 tbsp. almond butter; mix with water and ice cubes |
| **LUNCH** | 6 oz. grilled chicken breast, 1 1/2 cups jasmine rice, 1 cup steamed asparagus, 2 tbsp. olive oil, 1/2 avocado |
| **DINNER** | 6 oz. grilled salmon, 1 to 1 1/2 cups jasmine rice, 1 cup stir-fried vegetables, 1/2 avocado |

| TUESDAY | |
|---|---|
| **BREAKFAST** | Breakfast Shake: 1-2 scoops whey protein powder, 1 cup kale leaves, 1 cup raw steel cut oats, 1 cup frozen blueberries, 3 tbsp. unsweetened coconut flakes, 1 tsp. almond butter; mix with water and ice cubes |

| | |
|---|---|
| **LUNCH** | 6 oz. wild-caught fish, 1 1⁄2 cups baked sweet potatoes, 2 cups spinach salad, 2 tbsp. olive oil-based dressing, and 1/2 avocado |
| **DINNER** | 6 oz. grilled pork tenderloin, 1 cup mashed sweet potatoes, 1 cup steamed cauliflower with olive oil, and 1/2 avocado |

| **WEDNESDAY** | |
|---|---|
| **BREAKFAST** | Alpha Oats Breakfast – 1 cup cooked steel cut oats, 1 scoop whey protein, 1/2 cup blueberries, 1 sliced banana, 1 tbsp. almond butter |
| **LUNCH** | 6 oz. grilled chicken, 1 1/2 cups jasmine rice, 2 cups steamed broccoli with 1/2 avocado |
| **DINNER** | 6 oz. grass-fed steak, 1 cup mashed sweet potatoes with grass-fed butter, spinach salad with 1/2 avocado |

| **THURSDAY** | |
|---|---|
| **BREAKFAST** | Chocolate Cashew Oats Breakfast Bowl – 1 cup cooked steel cut oats, 1 scoop chocolate whey protein, 1/2 cup blackberries, 1/2 cup raspberries, 1 sliced banana, handful cashews |
| **LUNCH** | 6 oz. salmon grilled and served with 1 1/2 cups mashed sweet potatoes and 1 cup sautéed green beans with 1/2 avocado |
| **DINNER** | 1 can crab meat, 1/4 cup cooked steel cut oats, 1 whole egg, 1/2 diced onion, pan fried into a burger; serve with 1/2 cup jasmine rice, mustard, and steamed broccoli with 1/2 avocado |

| FRIDAY | |
|---|---|
| **BREAKFAST** | 1-2 scoops whey protein powder, 1 cup kale leaves, 1 cup raw steel cut oats, 1 tsp. almond butter, 1 cup frozen blueberries, 3 tbsp. unsweetened coconut flakes; mix with water and ice cubes |
| **LUNCH** | 6 oz. grilled chicken breast, 1 1/2 cups jasmine rice, 1 cup steamed asparagus, 2 tbsp. olive oil, 1/2 avocado |
| **DINNER** | 6 oz. grilled pork tenderloin, 1 cup mashed sweet potatoes, 1 cup steamed cauliflower with olive oil, and 1/2 avocado |

| SATURDAY | |
|---|---|
| **BREAKFAST** | 1 cup egg whites with 2-4 whole eggs scrambled with 1 cup diced vegetables, handful spinach and tomatoes fried in coconut oil; serve with 2 slices of Ezekiel bread, 1 avocado, and 1/2 cup berries on the side |
| **LUNCH** | 6 oz. grilled shrimp, 1 pita, 1 cup mixed greens, 1/2 sliced avocado, mustard, 1 cup blueberries |
| **DINNER** | 1 cup egg whites with 2 whole eggs scrambled with 1 cup diced vegetables in 1 tbsp. olive oil; serve with 1 cup pan-fried pre-baked sweet potatoes |

| SUNDAY | |
|---|---|
| **BREAKFAST** | 4 whole egg omelet, with spinach/kale, tomatoes, served with 3 pieces of turkey bacon with 2 slices of Ezekiel bread with grass-fed butter, and 1/2 avocado |
| **LUNCH** | 6 oz. grilled chicken, served with 2 slices Ezekiel bread, mustard, tomato, lettuce, and cucumber topped with 1/2 avocado; serve with 1 cup strawberries |
| **DINNER** | 6 oz. baked salmon with 1 cup mashed sweet potatoes and 1 cup green beans; serve with 1/2 avocado |

Now you have just about everything you need for a successful 28-day meal plan that will help you naturally boost your testosterone, lose weight, build muscle, and increase your energy levels. But let's add one more ingredient: success stories from real men who will inspire you to get started today and stay the course. Keep reading just a bit longer – you'll want to check out these guys' stories.

## SECTION 4

# Success Stories

**WELCOME TO THE SUCCESS STORIES** section of this book. This is where you'll find real-life accounts of men in my Over 40 Alpha Workout, Nutrition, and Brotherhood program that have used the Meta-Test Boost Nutrition System to achieve amazing health and fitness results.

From weight loss and muscle gain to increased testosterone, energy levels, and improved overall health, these stories will inspire and motivate you to take action toward your own health goals.

You'll read about the specific challenges these men faced, how they overcame them with the help of the MTB Nutrition System, and the specific benefits they achieved. These stories are proof that this plan – and lifestyle – is effective and can work for you too.

Get ready to be inspired to take your first step toward a healthier, fitter you.

### Arturo Had an Incredible Body, Health, and Life Transformation

Before embarking on his transformative journey with the Meta-Test Boost Nutrition System, Arturo's life had fallen into a detrimental routine. Each evening, he would return home from work, pop open a beer, and indulge in an array of unhealthy snacks and meals while watching television. This lifestyle led to poor sleep patterns, consistently low energy levels, and an increasingly irritable mood. He found himself trapped in a cycle of lethargy that negatively impacted his relationships, making him feel like an inadequate husband and father.

A layer of stubborn belly fat and weight gain only added to Arturo's woes, but he lacked the knowledge and direction necessary to make lasting changes. A family history of prostate cancer, heart disease, and diabetes served as a wake-up call. Arturo knew he needed to overhaul his diet and exercise regimen but had yet to discover the blueprint that would ultimately set him on the path to success.

Arturo's life underwent a remarkable transformation after he began using the Meta-Test Boost Nutrition System. He successfully shed an impressive 25 pounds, reducing his weight from 200 to 175 pounds. His pants size transitioned from a snug 34 to a comfortable 32, and his shirt size slimmed down from XL to L. Although he hadn't measured his body fat before starting the program, it now sits at a healthy 12.6 percent. Furthermore, Arturo's BMI made a significant leap from 29 to 23.

Feeling energized and more confident, Arturo rekindled his passion for surfing, enjoying improved performance in the water thanks to his newfound fitness. He also mastered the art of consistently maintaining a nutritious diet. These positive changes had a ripple effect on his personal life, as he became a better husband and father to his loved ones.

Under the Meta-Test Boost Nutrition System, Arturo noticed a heightened focus on exercise and nutrition. He stopped eating junk food and drinking beer, and he now rarely eats out. Driven to be a positive role model for his children, Arturo's ultimate goal is to lead a long, healthy life, hoping to one day witness the birth of his grandchildren.

Proud of his achievements, Arturo eagerly shares his experiences with friends and coworkers, inspiring them to embrace healthier lifestyles. He is a living testament to the power of perseverance, determination, and the right mindset and program to achieve success. In turn, he hopes to encourage his family to chase their dreams and goals, instilling in them the belief that, with the proper mindset, anything is possible.

### Abe's Journey to Boosted Testosterone and a Healthier Life

Meet Abe, a 51-year-old American who decided to take control of his health by embarking on a life-changing journey with the Meta-Test Boost Nutrition System. Before discovering this powerful nutrition plan, Abe's health had gradually declined, leading to a significant drop in his self-confidence.

Abe had always been committed to regular exercise, but as he entered his forties, he found that his usual workouts and eating habits were no longer producing the same results they did in his thirties. Despite attempting to maintain a healthy diet, Abe now realizes that it wasn't as beneficial as he once believed.

Four years ago, when Abe lost his job and canceled his gym membership to save money, his fitness journey took a turn for the worse. Although his apartment complex had a fitness room, he struggled to find the motivation to utilize it. As a result, he gained weight, reaching 206 pounds and 27 percent body fat. His self-confidence plummeted, and he resorted to wearing baggy clothing to hide his weight gain.

Determined to change his life, Abe joined the Brotherhood, seeking to lose fat, boost his energy levels, regain his self-confidence, and look good when out with his wife. After a year of commitment to the Meta-Test Boost Nutrition System, he dropped down to 180 pounds and achieved a lean 15 percent body fat, losing two pants sizes in the process.

But that wasn't all. Abe's testosterone levels, which had previously fluctuated between 445 ng/dL and 470 ng/dL, now sit at an impressive 605 ng/dL. Thanks to his weight loss, lean muscle gain, and boosted testosterone, Abe has regained his confidence and is enjoying life in the Alpha Zone. He can now comfortably wear clothes that had become too tight and revels in the increased energy that allows him to tackle life with renewed vigor.

Abe's story is a testament to the incredible potential of the Meta-Test Boost Nutrition System, demonstrating that it's never too late to transform your health and boost your testosterone levels.

### Alberto's Journey to Carb Enlightenment and Better Health

Alberto, a 49-year-old American, is proof of the transformative power of the Meta-Test Boost Nutrition System. With determination and the right guidance, he successfully turned his life around and now enjoys a healthier, more fulfilling lifestyle.

Before discovering the MTB Nutrition System, Alberto weighed 194 pounds and often felt tired and achy due to his rigorous gym routine. He sought weekly chiropractic treatments to address the pain, unaware of the importance of recovery, sleep, and mobility. Moreover, Alberto had been following a low-carb diet for a year, which had stunted his muscle growth and caused his health indicators, such as blood pressure and triglycerides, to rise.

Once he embraced the Meta-Test Boost Nutrition System and added way more carbs to his diet, Alberto began to experience remarkable results. He shed 12 pounds, slimming down to 182 pounds, and found that he needed new clothes to accommodate his leaner physique. Muscle growth and fat loss went hand in hand, thanks to the balanced nutritional approach of the program.

His health indicators, including blood pressure and triglycerides, now reflect above-average levels. Alberto's commitment to the Meta-Test Boost Nutrition System has moved him from dangerous diabetic levels to prediabetic levels. By incorporating a suitable amount of carbs into his diet, he improved his insulin sensitivity and achieved better overall health.

Today, Alberto exudes confidence, unafraid to remove his shirt when the opportunity arises. He now enjoys active vacations and plans to pursue even more adventures in the future.

Alberto attributes much of his success to the ability to easily stay focused on his nutrition, thanks to this simple-to-follow nutrition system. Since it's dedicated to a lifestyle instead of a diet, anyone can achieve their health and fitness goals.

### Anthony's Transformation: A Journey to Health and Confidence

Not long ago, Anthony's life was plagued by unhealthy eating habits, lack of exercise, and numerous failed attempts to lose weight. Tipping the scales at 205 pounds, he struggled to find the right path to better health. His biggest challenges were the poor food choices he made, combined with few workouts and misguided exercise routines. Fortunately, his brother's transformation using the Meta-Test Boost Nutrition System served as a wake-up call and the inspiration he needed to make a change.

Upon embracing the MTB Nutrition System, Anthony experienced rapid and impressive results. He lost 30 pounds, gained lean muscle mass, and boosted his testosterone and energy levels to heights he never thought possible. Now in the best shape of his life, Anthony's waist size shrank from 36-38 inches to a slim 33-34 inches, and he proudly wears medium-sized shirts.

His improved health extended beyond his physique, as Anthony's cholesterol and blood pressure reached perfect levels. His newfound energy, muscle, and confidence transformed not only his body but also his entire life. No longer self-conscious about his appearance, he enjoys going shirtless and has a newfound zest for life.

Anthony's happiness is evident, and he eagerly anticipates each workout session. Friends and family have taken notice of his remarkable transformation, and many now turn to him for advice on weight loss and muscle gain. Through the Meta-Test Boost Nutrition System, Anthony has embraced the plan's emphasis on consistency, willpower, and a never-give-up attitude, proudly living by the mantra, "No Excuses, No Fear."

### Ben's Remarkable Journey to Better Health

Ben, a 45-year-old Canadian brother, lost an incredible 42 pounds, dropped four pants sizes, and, more importantly, reclaimed his health and happiness.

Before embarking on his transformative journey, Ben weighed 236 pounds and faced numerous challenges. He suffered from constant back pain, low energy levels, and dissatisfaction with his appearance. With heart disease and high blood pressure running in his family, Ben knew it was only a matter of time before these health issues caught up with him. A heat rash incident where his belt buckle dug into his abdomen prompted him to take action and turn his life around.

Embracing the Meta-Test Boost Nutrition System, Ben's life underwent a stunning transformation. He now weighs 194 pounds, which he feels is the right weight for him. The positive changes are not just limited to his weight; he feels better overall, enjoying increased energy levels and less pain.

Ben's waist size went from 37 to 33 inches, and he's on the verge of fitting into size 32 pants. The additional energy has enabled him to be more active and engaged with his family and household tasks. No longer held back by fatigue, he is more motivated than ever to continue improving his well-being.

Ben's success with the MTB Nutrition System goes beyond just his physical health. It has inspired him to pursue a healthier lifestyle and motivated him to excel in all aspects of his life. This incredible transformation is a testament to the power of determination, support, and the right nutritional guidance.

## Bob's Incredible Journey: Boosting Testosterone and Shedding Body Fat

Meet Bob, a 50-year-old Texan who, through hard work and the right nutrition plan, managed to increase his testosterone levels, drop his body fat percentage to an impressive 13 percent (down from 22 percent), and comfortably fit into size 32 pants.

Before discovering the Meta-Test Boost Nutrition System, Bob had gained a significant amount of weight during the COVID-19 pandemic. He felt sluggish and was unhappy with his appearance in his son's wedding photos. Determined to make a change, Bob refused to buy larger clothes and, instead, set out to find a solution that would work for him at his age. That's when he came across my Over 40 Alpha Workout, Nutrition, and Brotherhood program and started using the Meta-Test Boost Nutrition System.

The results of Bob's dedication and commitment to the nutrition system and program have been astounding. He has successfully increased his testosterone levels, lost 40 pounds (going from 230 to 190 pounds), and reduced his pants size from a 36 waist to a 32.

Thanks to the boost in testosterone levels and the comprehensive nutrition plan, Bob now feels he is in the best shape of his life. His story stands as an inspiration to others, proving that age is no barrier when it comes to achieving an incredible health and fitness transformation.

## From Keto Struggles to Building Muscle: Brandon's Nutrition and Fitness Story

Meet 49-year-old Brandon who overcame numerous challenges before finding success using the Meta-Test Boost Nutrition System. His inspiring journey has seen him settle at a healthy weight, regain his libido, build more muscle, and achieve sound sleep.

Before turning to this nutrition plan, Brandon had been following the keto diet for two years and had lost a significant amount of weight, going from 223 pounds to a skinny 161 pounds in just eight months. However, he struggled to maintain his body fat levels due to the extreme weight loss, which included muscle loss.

When he transitioned to using the MTB Nutrition System, he added carbs back into his diet after learning about their potential to support testosterone levels, but he was initially afraid of the change.

Despite his fear, Brandon decided to take the leap into the nutrition program, and, since then, has transformed his life. Although he's still perfecting his nutrition, he has seen tremendous results. Brandon's weight increased to 190 pounds as he built muscle, and, after participating in a Funk Workout Challenge, he settled at a healthy 183 pounds.

Today, Brandon is stronger than ever before. His libido has improved, his sleep is more restful, and he has witnessed noticeable muscle growth in his shoulders and arms.

Brandon's journey is a testament to the importance of understanding and embracing the right nutrition for one's body. His dedication and willingness to experiment with his diet have paid off, leading to an incredible transformation that has left him healthier and stronger than ever before.

### Brett's Journey: Transforming Health, Boosting His Testosterone Levels, Shedding 12 Percent Body Fat, and Inspiring Change

Check out this amazing story about Brett who has transformed not only his own life but also the lives of those around him.

Brett had a high-pressure career as a private investigator, managing over 1,000 staff members. Stress was a constant presence in his life. Although he worked out six days a week, he realized he was overtraining, which left him feeling worn out and tired. In addition, his total cholesterol level had skyrocketed to 307, which became a significant concern after a colleague suffered a heart attack at age 52.

Brett knew he needed a change, and that's when he found the Meta-Test Boost Nutrition System and my Over 40 Alpha Workout, Nutrition, and Brotherhood program. Since joining, his body fat has dropped from 28 percent to an impressive 15 percent, and his testosterone levels have increased by 17 percent. His total cholesterol level plummeted from 307 to 170, a result that his doctor attributes to the combination of exercise, nutrition, and medication.

Throughout his journey, Brett has regained his lost athleticism and seen a significant improvement in his cardio fitness. He was delighted to find that his stamina on the stand-up paddleboard has vastly improved, even after a winter without practice. Additionally, the program's focus on nutrition helped him support his oldest daughter in her recovery from an eating disorder. The balanced plate approach and the principles taught in the program have made a lasting impact on his family.

Brett has become an inspiration to others, including his wife, who joined my Women's Alpha program after seeing his progress. He has also brought the concept of becoming 1 percent better every day into his workplace, aiming to instill this powerful mindset in his employees.

Brett's story is a testament to the life-changing power of the MTB Nutrition System. With determination, support, and the right tools, he has transformed his health, inspired others, and fostered an environment of growth and well-being in both his personal and professional life.

### Brian and Gracie's Incredible Journey: A Couple's Transformation

Next is a unique and inspiring success story of a husband-and-wife duo, Brian and Gracie. Together, they embraced the Meta-Test Boost Nutrition System and my program, not only transforming their bodies and health but also strengthening their relationship.

Before the MTB Nutrition System, Brian's unhealthy habits, combined with the stress of a 25-year law enforcement career, led him to gain weight, tipping the scales at 260 pounds. Gracie, a former dual-sport athlete, also struggled with body image due to the pressures of her law enforcement job. They tried to motivate each other to work out and become healthier, but the workouts Gracie created were too challenging for Brian, causing them to give up quickly.

But everything changed when they joined my program and started following this nutrition plan. The results speak for themselves. Brian began the program at 255 pounds and is now at 205, while Gracie went from 180 to 145 pounds. Brian's body fat percentage dropped by over 15 percent, and both of them now enjoy better health.

Brian's blood pressure, heart rate, and cholesterol have all significantly improved. His most recent cholesterol check showed a remarkable 62-point decrease compared to his pre-academy physical.

With a 34-inch waist, Brian now wears the same pants size he did when he graduated from the police academy in the best shape of his life. He feels like he has the strength and energy of his 25-year-old self, and he's amazed at the progress they've made together. This journey has not only helped Brian and Gracie transform their bodies and health, but it has also brought them closer as a couple.

Brian and Gracie's determination, commitment to the program, and unwavering support for each other have led them to achieve incredible results, setting an inspiring example for other couples who seek to transform their lives together.

### Cesar's Life-Changing Transformation: From Heart Attack Survivor to Thriving

Meet 52-year-old Cesar who turned his life around after a heart attack.

Before his health scare, Cesar struggled with poor eating habits, leading to apathy and weight gain. However, the heart attack was a wake-up call that prompted him to change his lifestyle for the sake of his health and his family.

After using the Meta-Test Boost Nutrition System, Cesar experienced measurable results. He shed 16 pounds, dropping from 268 to 252 pounds, and went from size 42 to size 38 pants. His stomach measurement decreased from 49 inches to 42 inches.

But the transformation goes beyond numbers. Since starting the nutrition plan, Cesar has discovered the importance of consistent exercise and its positive impact on his overall well-being. Most importantly, his commitment to a healthier lifestyle has resonated with his family, leading to a happier, more fulfilling life for everyone.

My "Get it done" mantra has become an integral part of Cesar's life, helping him tackle challenges with a renewed sense of determination. His attitude and mindset have changed dramatically since starting the program.

Cesar's advice to other men is to stick to the plan and keep pushing forward, even when feeling discouraged. He encourages everyone to lean on the supportive community in my program's Facebook group, as it provides motivation and valuable advice. With a focus on improving by 1 percent every day, Cesar reminds everyone to "Get it done!"

Cesar's transformation shows that with determination, commitment, and the support of a like-minded community it's possible to overcome even the toughest challenges and create a healthier, happier life for us and our loved ones.

### From Alcohol Dependency to Super Healthy: Chad's Remarkable Journey

I want to share Chad's incredible success story, detailing his transformation from alcohol dependency to a super healthy lifestyle thanks to the Meta-Test Boost Nutrition System.

Just a few months ago, Chad weighed 167 pounds and drank alcohol every day. As he embarked on his fitness journey, Chad soon discovered that a healthy diet is crucial for progress, as no amount of exercise can compensate for poor nutrition. After experiencing the negative effects of alcohol on his body when he allowed himself a drink, Chad realized that alcohol is a poison best avoided for optimal health and well-being. Quitting alcohol was the most challenging aspect of Chad's journey, even compared to the tough workouts.

Since he began using the Meta-Test Boost Nutrition System, Chad has dropped 17 pounds, bringing his weight down to a comfortable 150 pounds. More importantly, his relationships with his wife and daughter have improved significantly, as they are proud of the new Alpha Dad in their lives. Chad now finds his busy work and lifestyle more manageable, thanks to his ability to be more present and accountable.

Chad's story demonstrates the power of focusing on improving by 1 percent each day and making better choices. Remember, we are defined by our habits, which are fortunately within our control.

Chad's remarkable journey is a testament to the fact that with determination, support, and the right guidance anyone can overcome personal challenges and become the person they want to be.

### Conquering Sugar Cravings and Transforming His Life: Charles' Success Story

I want to share the inspiring success story of Charles, a 52-year-old Canadian who used the Meta-Test Boost Nutrition System to transform his body, health, and life while finally eliminating his sugar cravings.

Charles started struggling with his fitness journey after a hip resurfacing procedure in 2018. Unable to practice Brazilian jiu-jitsu and finding other exercises boring, he knew he needed a more focused and wholesome program that provided effective workouts and covered nutrition and recovery.

Through the Meta-Test Boost Nutrition System, Charles learned about the telltale signs of low testosterone, such as belly fat, low libido, and low energy. This realization made it clear that he needed to make a change for his well-being, and with the extra time provided by working from home during the pandemic, he decided to give the MTB Nutrition System a try.

Since using the nutrition system, Charles has lost an impressive 30 pounds and dropped five belt holes. In consultation with his doctor, he has been able to reduce his blood pressure medication, as his resting heart rate dropped below 40 beats per minute at night due to his weight loss.

Moreover, Charles' weight loss has cured his sleep apnea and snoring, eliminating the need for his CPAP machine. The most significant win for him, however, has been the continuous, incremental improvement in his overall health.

My nutrition regimen has also made a massive difference in Charles' life. Previously, he was constantly hungry, didn't eat carbs, and starved himself while still being overweight. But with the MTB Nutrition System meal plans, Charles is amazed at how much he can eat while maintaining a balanced diet and continuing to lose weight. The program has also helped him conquer his sugar cravings, which are now extremely rare.

Charles' fantastic achievements and continual progress toward a healthier and happier life is a testament to how, with the right system, individuals can transform their lives for the better!

### Revitalizing Energy and Transforming Life: David's Success Story

Meet David, a 51-year-old British brother who has regained his runner's body and revitalized his energy levels by using the Meta-Test Boost Nutrition System.

Just a few months ago, David was struggling with his weight and energy levels, even though he was an avid runner of 10k races and sub two-hour half marathons. At 73 kilograms and with a BMI of over 26, he found that the strategies that had worked for him when he was younger were no longer effective. David felt stuck in his training and race times and was unhappy with his physique and mindset, lacking a plan to turn his life around.

The Meta-Test Boost Nutrition System and my workout programs have been a game-changer for David. In just 90 days, he has lost 6 kilograms (13 pounds), reduced his body fat to 20 percent, and gained muscle in his upper body, particularly in his shoulders, biceps, chest, and lats. His core has become stronger, and he is now on the path to revealing his six-pack. Moreover, David's legs have grown stronger, enhancing his running speed and endurance.

David credits the nutrition component of the program as the key to his success. By changing his diet and resetting his metabolism, he has seen a significant increase in energy levels, and his digestive system has improved dramatically. Cutting sugar from his diet has also made him feel fantastic.

In addition to the physical benefits, David has embarked on a journey of self-improvement. He has been working on building self-awareness to identify and eliminate the bad habits that were holding him back. He is now committed to being a better man every day, with more courage and love for life.

David's remarkable progress is a testament to the power of adopting a life-changing nutrition system, which can help individuals transform their lives and reach their full potential for themselves, their families, and their communities.

CONCLUSION

# Taking Control of Your Health and Fitness

**THE META-TEST BOOST NUTRITION SYSTEM** is a comprehensive and powerful strategy to take control of your health and fitness. By incorporating key nutritional elements and healthy habits, you will be able to optimize your physical performance, mental well-being, and overall vitality – and unlock your full potential.

Embracing the MTB Nutrition System's principles involves consuming a well-rounded diet, rich in micronutrients and macronutrients that support increased testosterone, fat loss, hormonal balance, muscle growth, energy, and recovery.

Additionally, it is essential to maintain a consistent exercise routine tailored to your personal goals and abilities, ensuring a harmonious balance between metabolic training, muscle building, and strength training.

Alongside these crucial factors, prioritizing sleep quality and stress management while incorporating adequate hydration will help you achieve a healthy lifestyle that supports your health and fitness journey.

As you progress, remember to be patient, listen to your body, and adjust your routine as needed.

Surrounding yourself with a support network of friends, family, or professionals can provide the encouragement and resources needed to stay on track. For additional support on your health and fitness journey, consider joining my Over 40 Alpha Workout, Nutrition, and Brotherhood program. (Learn more at www.over40Alpha.com .)

Above all, remember that adopting the Meta-Test Boost Nutrition System is a commitment to your long-term well-being and an investment in your future.

By embracing these principles and remaining consistent, you will not only transform your physique but also enjoy increased energy, enhanced mental clarity, and improved quality of life. Take control of your health and fitness today, and reap the benefits of a happier, healthier, and more empowered you.

# Science and Research References

1. Habito, Raymundo C., et al. "Effects of Replacing Meat with Soybean in the Diet on Sex Hormone Concentrations in Healthy Adult Males." *British Journal of Nutrition* 84.4 (2000): 557-563.

2. Hämäläinen, E. K., et al. "Decrease of Serum Total and Free Testosterone During a Low-Fat High-Fibre Diet." *Journal of Steroid Biochemistry* 18.3 (1983): 369-370.

3. Volek, Jeff S., et al. "Effects of a High-Fat Diet on Postabsorptive and Postprandial Testosterone Responses to a Fat-Rich Meal." *Metabolism – Clinical and Experimental* 50.11 (2001): 1351-1355.

4. Lane, Amy R., Joseph W. Duke, and Anthony C. Hackney. "Influence of Dietary Carbohydrate Intake on the Free Testosterone: Cortisol Ratio Responses to Short-Term Intensive Exercise Training." *European Journal of Applied Physiology* 108.6 (2010): 1125-1131.

5. Oi-Kano, Yuriko, et al. "Oleuropein Supplementation Increases Urinary Noradrenaline and Testicular Testosterone Levels and Decreases Plasma Corticosterone Level in Rats Fed High-Protein Diet." *The Journal of Nutritional Biochemistry* 24.5 (2013): 887-893.

6. Prasad, Ananda S., et al. "Zinc Status and Serum Testosterone Levels of Healthy Adults." *Nutrition Journal* 12.5 (1996): 344-348.

7. Pilz, S., et al. "Effect of Vitamin D Supplementation on Testosterone Levels in Men." *Hormone and Metabolic Research* 43.3 (2011): 223.

8. Meikle, A. Wayne, Xan-Hua Liu, and John D. Stringham. "Extracellular Calcium and Luteinizing Hormone Effects on 22-Hydroxycholesterol Used for Testosterone Production in Mouse Leydig Cells." *Journal of Andrology* 12.2 (1991): 148-151.

9. Naghii, M. R., and S. Samman. "The Effect of Boron on Plasma Testosterone and Plasma Lipids in Rats." *Nutrition Research* 17.3 (1997): 523-531.

10. Peyreigne, Christelle, et al. "Effect of Hydration on Exercise-Induced Growth Hormone Response." *European Journal of Endocrinology* 145.4 (2001): 445-450.

11. Demark-Wahnefried, Wendy, et al. "Pilot Study of Dietary Fat Restriction and Flaxseed Supplementation in Men with Prostate Cancer before Surgery: Exploring the Effects on Hormonal Levels, Prostate-Specific Antigen, and Histopathologic Features." *Urology* 58.1 (2001): 47-52.

12. Akdogan, Mehmet, et al. "Effects of Peppermint Teas on Plasma Testosterone, Follicle-Stimulating Hormone, and Luteinizing Hormone Levels and Testicular Tissue in Rats." *Urology* 64.2 (2004): 394-398.

13. Van Thiel, David H., et al. "Alcohol-Induced Testicular Atrophy in the Adult Male Rat." *Endocrinology* 105.4 (1979): 888-895.

14. Meikle, A. Wayne. "The Interrelationships between Thyroid Dysfunction and Hypogonadism in Men and Boys." *Thyroid* 14.3, Supplement 1 (2004): 17-25.

15. Hartmann, S., Lacorn, M., and Steinhart, H. (2008). "Natural Occurrence of Steroid Hormones in Food." *Food and Chemical Toxicology* 46(6), 1806-1818. doi: 10.1016/j.fct.2007.09.096

16. Sarkola, T., and Adlercreutz, H. (1994). "Reduced Plasma Testosterone Level in Alcoholics with Cirrhosis." *Addiction Biology* 39(3), 365-369.

17. Välimäki, M., Tuominen, J. A., Huhtaniemi, I., Ylikahri, R., and Penttilä, I. M. (1984). "The Pulsatile Secretion of Gonadotropins and Testosterone and the Rate of Testicular Steroidogenesis are Reduced by Ethanol in Man." *Journal of Clinical Endocrinology & Metabolism* 58(6), 1075-1081.

18. Vignera, S., Condorelli, R. A., Balercia, G., Vicari, E., and Calogero, A. E. (2013). "Does Alcohol Have Any Effect on Male Reproductive Function? A Review of Literature." *Asian Journal of Andrology* 15(2), 221-225.

19. Hull, E. M., & Dominguez, J. M. (2007). "Sexual Behavior in Male Rodents." *Hormones and Behavior* 52(1), 45-55.

# Dedication

**TO ALL MY BROTHERS** in our Over 40 Alpha Workout, Nutrition, and Brotherhood program who embraced the Meta-Test Boost Nutrition System to transform their bodies, health, and life while naturally increasing their testosterone. You are an inspiration to me 365 days a year, #GID!

# Acknowledgments

**THIS BOOK IS DEDICATED** to God Almighty, Jesus Christ my Lord and Savior, and the Holy Spirit who guides each day.

My beautiful wife, Angela Roberts, who is my Queen and best friend, for being by my side and giving me unconditional love during this entire writing process.

My amazing son, Cassian, you are truly becoming the epitome of the strong, smart, and savage Alpha Man that I wish I was at your age!

My mother and father! Thanks G-Ro for our daily FaceTime talks and your daily *love* that keeps me going each day. Thanks, Crofter, you are a *legend*!

To my biggest and #1 fan sister, Charlotte B.

My incredible and loving cats Fairtex and Yodsenski, you are both an amazing stress relief!

To my mother-in-law, Pat B., for taking the cats whenever we travel and helping out in other ways too.

To my awesome niece Mikayla…thanks for those amazing cottage workouts and meals

To all my family, cousins, aunts, and uncles for your support.

Team Funk HQ, I want you to always remember I would not be where I am today without your help: Mike, Rick (The Twins), Estella, Sarah, Irshad, Andy T., Jonathan, Kadesha, Waqas, Dexter, Flex, Andrea, Gregory, Jeff, Kara, Shannon, Marianne, Vanessa, Tyler, Brian, and David.

To the Super Twins for helping me resurrect the Funk Roberts mission and Over 40 Brand and Tribe Secrets.

To Rory and the team at VidApp for helping me create my Funk Fitness Shred App.

To my supplement company, Funk Supplements Inc., and the crew at Ship Central and Canadian Premiere Supplements.

To my supplement partner, Dr. Stephen Anton, for the journey of creating Alpha Max Test 3D – Testosterone Booster.

To James L., awesome copywriter.

Thank You so much to Dawn Bowman for the cover picture of the book and all the great work you have done with me in the past

To *all* my Funk Fitness University students, thank you for spreading health and fitness to men over 40 and the world.

And to everyone else in my life who has helped to make this book truly happen.

To my sponsor, Roger S., for helping me live a clean and serene life!

A MASSIVE FUNK ROBERTS THANKS to all my Over 40 Alpha Brothers who live by this book, who live the Alpha Male code, and for changing their lives and showing that, no matter how old you are, you can be in the best shape and health of your life in your 40s, 50, 60s, and beyond!

# About the Author

**AS A FORMER PROFESSIONAL ATHLETE,** Funk Roberts knows how to train at the highest levels, mentally and physically. Today, Funk is an online fitness entrepreneur who successfully runs two seven-figure businesses.

Recognized as a leading international fitness expert, he is the creator of Funk Roberts Fitness Inc. and Funk Supplements. Notably, he is also the creator of the Over 40 Alpha Workout, Nutrition, and Brotherhood program, a monthly membership program with more than 14,000 members, dedicated to helping men around the world revitalize their health and fitness. Specifically, Funk's program guides men to naturally increase their testosterone levels while transforming their overall health through new monthly workouts, nutritional information, exclusive products, motivating programs, and a supportive community of "brothers."

Funk is a recipient of the 2-Comma Club Award through ClickFunnels for generating $1 million in one year using one funnel. In 2022, he was awarded the prestigious Presenter of the Year Award from CanFitPro – the largest provider of education in the Canadian fitness industry. CanFitPro recently invited him to serve on its board, where he will advise on new programs and products, serve as an ambassador, and be a voice of authority for the media.

Always striving to advance his knowledge, Funk currently attends Harvard Business School Online part-time where he is pursuing a certificate in Entrepreneurship and Innovation.

Funk is a Certified Master Metabolic Trainer, Certified MMA Conditioning Coach (MMACA)-NESTA, Certified Fitness Nutrition Coach, Core Conditioning Specialist-NESTA, Kettlebell Training Specialist, Pain-Free Performance Specialist, and Mindset Coach.

He has partnered with the National Exercise and Sports Trainers Association (NESTA) to create and launch his Metabolic Conditioning Coach Certification Course, which teaches and certifies personal/bootcamp trainers and coaches using HIIT and metabolic training. This course has become the most popular certification in the NESTA library. Funk and his wife, Angela Roberts, also work for UFC Canada, Australia, and New Zealand with Athlete Relations and Operations where they are part of the team that is responsible for all fighters during fight week.

Funk is a two-time Amazon #1 Best-Selling Author for *Over 40 Shred* and *Rapid Body Makeover.* He has appeared as a fitness and celebrity expert on ABC, NBC, CBS, and FOX TV affiliates and has been featured in *GQ*, *Muscle & Fitness*, *Train Magazine*, *Inside Fitness Magazine*, *Men's Journal*, *Status Fitness Magazine*, *Yahoo Health*, *Healthline*, and others. Funk is also coauthor of the forthcoming book *Mission Driven,* published by Celebrity Press LLC. He was asked to coauthor this book due to his commitment to professional success and willingness to share his knowledge on creating a healthy lifestyle.

Funk is driven to help men completely transform their lives. With 720,000 subscribers on YouTube and over one million followers on Facebook, he is well on his way to achieving his goal to educate and empower one million men over the age of 40 on the importance of health and fitness for their lives, their families, and their communities by 2025.

Fueled by a deep commitment and passion, Funk led the effort to create National Testosterone Awareness Day, which is recognized annually on November 17. This day focuses on educating the public about testosterone and its importance in men's health.

Now in his 50s, Funk is happily married to Angela and has an older son, Cassian. They all have a passion for traveling the world, training Muay Thai in Thailand, and working with the UFC. Funk enjoys spending time online with his Over 40 Alpha Brothers and spending quality time with his family.

**Learn more at www.over40alpha.com**

Printed in Great Britain
by Amazon

29283130R00086